Center Stage

Library Programs That Inspire

Premiere Events: Library Programs That Inspire Elementary School Patrons. By Patricia Potter Wilson and Roger Leslie.

Igniting the Spark: Library Programs That Inspire High School Patrons. By Roger Leslie and Patricia Potter Wilson.

Center Stage: Library Programs That Inspire Middle School Patrons. By Patricia Potter Wilson and Roger Leslie.

Center Stage

Library Programs That Inspire Middle School Patrons

Patricia Potter Wilson

and

Roger Leslie

2002
Libraries Unlimited
A Division of Greenwood Publishing Group, Inc.
Greenwood Village, Colorado

LIBRARIES UNLIMITED
7730 East Belleview Avenue, Suite A200
Greenwood Village, CO 80111
1-800-225-5800
www.lu.com

Library of Congress Cataloging-in-Publication Data

Wilson, Patricia J. (Patricia Jane)
  Center stage : library programs that inspire middle school patrons / Patricia Potter Wilson and Roger Leslie.
    p. cm. -- (Library programs that inspire)
Includes bibliographical references and index.
    ISBN 1-56308-796-0
      1. Middle school libraries--Activity programs--United States. 2. Media programs (Education)--United States. I. Leslie, Roger. II. Title.

  Z675.S3 W7537 2002
  027.8'223—dc21

                                    2002003185

To Lee Mountain, my friend and mentor, who started me on the road to publishing.
Pat

To my mother, who teaches me daily how to savor life with palpable joy.
Roger

Contents

Chapter 5: HOW TO GATHER AND ORGANIZE RESOURCES (*continued*)

Chapter 6: SEARCHING THE INTERNET FOR RESOURCES. 99

Chapter 8: DYNAMIC MODEL PROGRAMS AND IDEAS (*continued*)

List of Illustrations

FIGURES

PHOTOGRAPHS

Acknowledgments

We are grateful to the media specialists, university professors, and friends who supported us throughout this project. First, we thank the 20 school library media specialists who provided the model programs and ideas that make up Chapter 8. That section brings to life every explanation throughout the text. Without their dynamic program ideas, this book could not have been written.

The professors in the School of Education at University of Houston-Clear Lake generously shared their time and knowledge. Holly Blaylock gave much time and energy to contribute the model program that runs throughout the chapters. Dr. Maureen White encouraged us throughout the project, and Ms. Ann Kimzey was there to advise us and proofread the manuscript. We particularly want to thank Julie Hardegree for the numerous hours she spent searching the Internet for outstanding Web sites and Mr. Isidro Grau for his technology advice.

Although many library media specialists were involved in this project, we extend a special thank-you to the University of Houston-Clear Lake students enrolled in school library internships. They worked diligently examining model programs in various school districts. We also thank Dr. Barry Bishop for his support throughout the project.

Finally, we thank Wendell Wilson, Debbie Potter Parker, Jerry Roberts, and Jerry and Richard Leslie for sharing our vision and enthusiasm for this project.

Introduction

The greatest challenge for middle school library media specialists—securing the interest of energetic, independent young patrons—also provides the strongest opportunity to shape lives and encourage lifelong learning. In elementary school, curriculum for media specialists is often dictated by the school or district. Library classes are incorporated into the school day; and media specialists act as independent teachers, taking on regular class loads with all the responsibilities and commitments of a classroom teacher. In this forum, students recognize the school library media center as an integral part of their learning environment, and hone the skills of reading, gathering information, and discovering what resources are available for independent learning. In general, elementary students either love the library or at least recognize its importance in their day-to-day learning.

By high school, students have already developed a clear, often rigid, opinion about the library media center. Except for their required involvement in specific, short-term research and independent reading projects, high-school students are either regular patrons or complete strangers to the facility.

Middle school, the pivotal transition between these two stages, cements patrons' attitudes about the school library media center. In these few years, they either develop an appreciation of the abundant learning opportunities and resources available, or they dismiss it as an onerous and frustrating area of school to avoid whenever possible.

Our first book in this series, *Premiere Events: Library Programs That Inspire Elementary School Patrons*, formed a natural blend of topic and audience: while enriching and supplementing the elementary curriculum, programs promote reading for learning and enjoyment. Our second book, *Igniting the Spark: Library Programs That Inspire High School Patrons*, required its own focus: enticing all students into the media center by creating programs that capture the imagination of not only the naturally inquisitive, but also the stubbornly disinterested.

But for middle school, an entirely new, yet very promising, challenge arises. In this precarious stage of personal and educational development, middle-school students are ripe for change and open to new views. Given the freedom of a new, less rigidly scheduled use of the school library media center, and not yet independent enough to decide concretely whether they consider the media center a kaleidoscope of engaging learning opportunities or a dungeon of antiquated dust-collectors, middle-school students are perhaps the most impressionable group. They can be wowed into recognizing the vibrant power of the media center, or jaded into associating all media centers with academia so stuffy that even our future "Einsteins" would rather surf the Net at home than step one foot across our threshold.

What kinds of activities could possibly shape positive opinions for students of any learning style and all achievement levels? Programming. Naively, I once perceived programs as rare, sometimes unworkable additions to my daily responsibilities. They are not.

Instead, programs can be any activities, great or small, that support learning and encourage patrons to use the school library media center.

As my co-author and I learned by surveying middle school library media specialists throughout the country, and as we hope you will discover from their contributions to this book, library programs are not infrequent events that drain already over-extended media specialists. Instead, just as they do at the elementary and high school levels, library programs invigorate, expand, and enrich the school library media center's role in education. And just as important, they often distinguish the most successful specialists at award-winning middle schools (many of whom contributed program ideas to this text) from media specialists slowly burning out from the new responsibilities that global education has demanded of us all.

Library programming is as integral to the profession as circulation, research, and administration. Surprisingly, however, between my first book on programming, *Happenings: Developing Successful Programs for School Libraries*, and our previous two books in this series, very few publications have even addressed the topic exclusively.

Libraries Unlimited suggested that we write a series of books on this topic, long in need of representation on our professional shelves. While my co-author and I share a career background as school library media specialists, our unique contributions to the work come from diverse experiences in the field.

As a lifelong educator, Roger Leslie has enjoyed much first-hand experience motivating students to learn. His work as a secondary school library media specialist focused primarily on programming as a way to reach students. Constant interaction with his young adult patrons helped shape the characterizations of his forthcoming novel *Drowning in Secret* (Absey & Co., 2002) and the activities in his forthcoming motivational book for teens, *The Success Express* (Bayou, 2002). Further, being a YA book reviewer for *Booklist* has provided him firsthand knowledge of resource topics of interest to middle school and high school patrons and keeps him apprised of publishing trends.

Before earning my doctorate in education, I was an elementary school teacher and library media specialist. During that time, I filled my classroom and then my school library media center with special events, educational activities, and resources to excite students about special topics and encourage them to read and learn. As a university professor of school library science courses, I emphasized program development, even adding a programming component to both the school library administration course and the internship. In addition to my research on professional collections and the development of *The Professional Collection of Elementary Educators* (H. W. Wilson, 1986), I am nationally recognized for my efforts to add a school library component to graduate courses for aspiring school principals.

In this book, we offer detailed information for planning, executing, and assessing school library programs; emphasize the benefits of such programs; and share winning program ideas developed and carried out by middle school media specialists at award-winning schools across the nation. (Chapter 8 describes the programs in detail.) We also incorporate numerous program ideas throughout the text. When sharing original suggestions submitted by only one professional, we credit that person by name. When including identical or overlapping ideas from more than one school library media specialist, we combine them for clarity and create a name or description.

We genuinely believe that programming is one of the most effective tools available to media specialists. The benefits of programming are extensive and long lasting. Programming promotes lifelong reading and learning. It supports and enriches curriculum. It can encourage consistent, loyal patronage by students and faculty. Perhaps most important, it advertises and promotes the school library media center, making an impression on the student body, your colleagues, and the entire community of which your facility is an essential part. By suggesting topics, leading you to appropriate resources, and explaining the step-by-step process of executing program plans, we hope to inspire you to bring your middle-school patrons center stage through programming.

CHAPTER BY CHAPTER PREVIEW

Using an example from a dynamic middle school media specialist known for ingenious programs that comprise the core of all her professional goals, Chapter 1 introduces a model program that we trace, stage-by-stage, throughout the text. Following this example we offer an extensive working definition of library programming, both determining exactly what constitutes a program, and distinguishing the term *library program* in this context from its generic reference to all duties required of media specialists. Chapter 1 also discusses various types of programs and describes their benefits.

Chapter 2 describes several options for planning a library program. Because these initial steps support all subsequent stages, good planning is essential to a program's success. Beyond traditional ways of determining student interest and selecting a theme, we also share unique ideas from several library media specialists that enhance the process.

Chapter 3 explains effective strategies for gathering and organizing program information. Whether your program is a simple interactive display or an elaborate, weeklong event, careful planning and meticulous organization ensure the greatest benefits for audiences and the least frustration for you.

After completing initial program planning, you will need access to the most useful information, resources, and support staff available. Chapter 4 shares suggestions for identifying and locating hard-to-find resources; and Chapter 5 provides successful approaches for recruiting and instructing volunteers, and organizing material resources for current and future use.

The global focus on our profession has created some often-overwhelming responsibilities. But with them has come access to information as we have never seen before. Consequently, Chapter 6 offers a list of some of the best Internet sites related to school subjects and topics of interest to young adults that can be used to plan programs and extend student learning following the event.

As with any project, assessment and evaluation are essential for determining what works effectively and what needs revision. Chapter 7 recommends various assessment tools and sample evaluations for determining your program strengths and weaknesses. Perhaps even more helpful are the subsequent suggestions for enhancing successful programs that you may want to repeat, refining good ideas that initially did not result in a strong program, or eliminating programs that no longer meet student needs and interests.

Chapter 8 opens the creative floodgates with outstanding sample programs from library media specialists throughout the United States. Covering an array of topics across the curriculum, these innovative, entertaining, and effective programs showcase colleagues at the height of their creativity. You may host these exact programs on your campus, or tailor the details to the precise needs of your school population.

Throughout, we aspire to do more than merely generate interest in library programming. Rather, we hope to supply you with tools for reaching more middle-school students and affecting them more deeply than you have before. No one in our profession needs more work. However, we could use a new vision for generating interest in students who resist reading or hold negative stereotypes of the media center and the people who run it. While no single philosophy will magically enhance an entire profession, the new vision we espouse can certainly spark your creativity and tap student potential as you keep them center stage in your pursuit of professional excellence.

CHAPTER 1

Putting Students Center Stage

Even in this global learning environment that divides our energies and scatters our focus, we must ensure that student success remains the primary goal of all educators. For classroom teachers, that objective continues to be central to everything they do. The lesson plans they create, the units they teach, and the tests they develop and grade are all directly aligned with that purpose.

As library media specialists, we are presented with an extra challenge. On one level, we do work directly with students. We help them research and we provide them with strategies for independent learning. We help them select resources to meet their class assignment needs as well as their personal interests. We guide their Internet searches, teach them technical skills, monitor their behavior, encourage their success, or re-explain what they may not have understood when their teacher first presented the lesson. From this perspective, we are able to keep students our central focus.

Many of our behind-the-scenes activities indirectly serve the same purpose. In addition to selecting, ordering, processing, and shelving books so our student patrons will have great resources, we must make sure those resources are available in different formats, create an inviting atmosphere in our school library media center, and keep track of materials so they are available for that proverbial teachable moment.

As if all these demands aren't enough to keep us busy, it is also our job to serve the needs of the entire faculty. We must be ready in an instant for teachers who need overhead projector bulbs changed, want a particular resource, or need to schedule a last-minute visit to the library media center. Similarly, administrators depend on us to provide equipment for school events, take leadership roles on campus committees, and realign daily schedules to accommodate standardized testing or large meetings with visiting administrators.

With so many responsibilities, it is no wonder that many library media specialists get so consumed by the peripheral demands of their job that they sometimes lose contact with the very core of their profession. At the very least, we want to educate students. At best, we want to introduce them to the endless possibilities for learning and encourage a love of reading.

Keeping or recapturing that vision does not demand changing professions or learning new educational strategies. It merely requires you to find a way to keep students center stage. That way is through library programming.

MEDIA CENTER
PROGRAMMING DEFINED

In general, a program can be almost any special event that presents information in an effective format. While meeting specific learning objectives, it also encourages students to learn more about a topic and to explore their interest in it following the event. Programs generally require completing three steps before the event (planning, organizing, and promoting) and an equally important step afterward (assessing). Under this broad description of programs are myriad program types, ranging from simple displays or one-speaker presentations to elaborate weeklong events open to the school population and the community.

In any form, media center programs are created to serve the needs of students and faculty members. Done well, they will simultaneously engender positive attitudes about school library media centers, encourage patrons to frequent the media center more often, and increase the use and circulation of resources. Although media specialists usually call the entire body of their work responsibility their "school library media center program," throughout this text the words "program" or "programming" refer exclusively to special events and activities created by media specialists, either alone or collaboratively with faculty members.

TYPES OF PROGRAMS

For many media specialists, programming's greatest appeal is its flexibility. Programs have very few constraints. They require only three components: (1) a clear learning objective, (2) a plan for presenting information, and (3) assessment strategies to gauge the lesson's effectiveness. Within the parameters of these three elements, you are free to develop programs of any type, format, and theme through any creative presentation you prefer.

Exhibits and Displays

Your school library media center may contain standard displays or even multifaceted exhibits. A freestanding book display and eye-catching bulletin board combine to make one of the most common types of program. Changed monthly, seasonally, or only when new books arrive, simple displays draw attention and personalize the atmosphere of your school library media center. But displays need not remain simple. Some of the greatest programs are displays that highlight your unique creativity. From three-dimensional wall decorations to interactive bulletin boards, displays are effective learning tools that middle-school students often love.

Displays can be the focal point of a program or an enhancing supplement. Books on related topics or themes can come to life with the support of an intriguing title splashed across a bulletin board, by charts or pictures relating to the books' subjects, or even exhibit items that can be used as manipulatives, or, if valuable, arranged in a locked display case. Occasionally, artifacts or mementos shared by teachers or rented from local museums can enliven topics more vividly than photographs and handouts. While protected, materials may be left out longer, or rearranged and added to for long-term interest. Depending on the display format and the relevance of the topic, some displays can appropriately be left up for extended periods of time, with items and books either remaining the same or changed and updated as book circulation wavers or as the focus of a particular unit shifts over time.

You, teachers, or even students can construct effective exhibits. If your budget allows, you may also rent or purchase them from sources beyond campus. (Some of those sources are mentioned in Chapter 4.) Exhibits can even enhance guest speakers' presentations or reinforce a research topic. If a teacher asks to display student projects in the school library media center after a unit, competition, or fair, let them be more than mere decoration. Add a learning component such as a fact sheet or an interactive quiz or game to make it a self-contained program.

Arranging topic-related library books near the exhibit is the easiest way to add a library-learning element. But other, equally effective, possibilities are also available. Listing a reference book bibliography and an Internet Webography under the heading "For Further Reading" invites curious students to continue learning independently.

Featured Speakers and Entertainers

Programs centering around guest speakers are among the most effective teaching tools available. Like elementary school media specialists, you may frequently invite guests to share information or skills with students. With guest speakers, your primary responsibility is to accommodate their needs. Because they generally bring their own materials, they often need you to provide only the space and, occasionally, the equipment to make their presentations.

Your guests need not be professionals who speak on their topic for a living. There are experts all around you. For example, rather than requiring students to look in reference books for information on gemstones, invite a jeweler to speak about the subject. Instead of giving booktalks on several new resources about sports, ask a current or retired professional athlete to share stories and answer questions for a target audience. As support, provide handouts (your speaker may supply them) and have resources on the topic available for student checkout.

Schoolwide career days, book fairs, and multicultural festivals are common annual events in middle schools. But guest speakers who share personal information relating to core curriculum, electives, or general interest add unique, sometimes rare dimensions to the students' learning.

Interest Centers

Once a staple in elementary school classrooms only, interest centers are now being used by media specialists at all levels. From simple centers arranged on tables or study carrels to elaborate partitioned areas that can accommodate several small groups simultaneously, interest centers invite interactive learning that students can pursue at their own pace.

Like displays, interest centers need not be static. They can begin small and grow over time. One library media specialist developed an interest center by displaying science and astronomy books, maps of the universe, and special effects videos around *Star Wars* trivia cards. Over time, the collection and a game evolved. The media specialist displayed authentic *Star Wars* memorabilia in a locked case, including a lunch box, movie script, photographs, toys, and collectibles either purchased or donated by students.

The game, which eventually became a schoolwide contest to win some of the displayed memorabilia, branched into three different categories: (1) science, (2) astronomy, and (3) *Star Wars* movies. To win some of the display memorabilia, students had to answer questions from each of the three categories, in that order. As a result, the *Star Wars* experts had to search for and brush up on their science and astronomy knowledge in order to move on to the questions about the movies they knew so well. The memorabilia prizes and a general competitiveness among *Star Wars* fans fueled the competition long enough to keep the exhibit displayed for most of a semester.

Demonstrations

Instead of giving an oral presentation, facilitators can demonstrate a process. Students (especially kinesthetic learners) favor demonstrations because they encourage interaction with the teacher, the guest facilitator, or you. This hands-on approach allows the instructor to give a demonstration while students observe, ask questions, and then model the technique themselves. Demonstrations work as independent activities, or as one component of a larger, multifaceted program. In either context, they appeal to curious, energetic students.

Media

Although media are often used to support programs such as guest speaker presentations, entire events can be planned exclusively around a video, multimedia presentation, recording, or computer program. Because it mirrors recreational activities such as watching television or playing computer games, this program format attracts and holds the attention of program participants. Media can serve as both the primary teaching tool and the program topic. For example, you may help students create PowerPoint presentations or teach faculty members how to navigate a new research database. Because teachers need to master computer skills and many students require fast-paced, multi-image formats to keep their attention, media programs are especially effective.

PROGRAM FOCUS

The focus for your program can vary as much as program types. Sometimes, the focus can even determine the type of program you present. Choosing your focus—the purpose of your program—allows you to develop ideas that support the learning objectives for your target audience.

Programs Based on Curriculum

Frequently, you may select program topics based on curricular needs. Whether offered to develop research skills or to teach learning objectives for a particular subject area, programs based on curriculum are among the most diverse and relevant. If you are not required to teach daily library classes like your elementary school colleagues, then you're free to develop curriculum-based programs that target specific student needs. When not constrained by bulleted objectives in a curriculum guide, you can capitalize on meaningful, teachable moments by creating programs that meet the immediate needs of students. Over time, you can modify and adapt such programs so long as they continue to meet curriculum requirements.

Elaborate programs built around curriculum are also versatile. You can vary your activities and repeat programs year after year. As any teacher knows, the same approach does not necessarily inspire different classes the same way. In the future, you might modify larger programs to address the needs of new groups, and to enrich and supplement curriculum. As curriculum demands change, you can adapt new approaches and find new inspirations for developing programs that relate to classroom learning.

Programs Based on Target Groups

You may also develop a program by first choosing a specific audience. Groups from the smallest gifted and talented classes to entire grade levels or departments may inspire program ideas. Because many skills apply to a vast cross-section of the student population, planning a program by first choosing a target group enables you to customize your program to their unique needs.

Target groups may vary greatly in size or type. Common choices include different ages, subject areas, and extracurricular groups. But just as relevant, and sometimes even more inspiring, are program ideas designed for more unique groups. For an English as a Second Language (ESL) group, a media specialist in Texas invited a dance troupe all the way from New Orleans to perform for the students. Finding a group that could demonstrate or perform its skills without the language barrier being much of a hindrance inspired her to continue such programs in the future. For subsequent programs, the media specialist invited a magician, a jazz music ensemble, and a mariachi band. All shared their talents in a format that these students with limited English proficiency could appreciate and learn.

Target groups do not have to be this specialized, and the programs don't need to be repeated in different contexts in the future. Target audiences might be specific classes, entire grade levels, or certain populations (such as gifted and talented, the Spanish Club, or special education students). Whoever the program audience, contour your topic to their educational or personal development needs.

Programs Based on Special Themes

Because its parameters are so specific, a thematic program can be the easiest to develop. Whether the theme is inspired by district requirements (multicultural or technology fairs) or special events (World Series or Olympics), programs based on special themes invite creative exploration and development. Best of all, this creative freedom includes not having to focus too long on making logistical decisions (for example, which groups to invite) because many of these decisions are dictated by the theme itself.

Because the theme usually determines the what and when of the program, you can spend your planning time finding the most fun, effective way to present the theme. Impressed by a "Bring a Pet Photo to School" activity that was sponsored by a colleague, a media specialist in California expanded the theme into the school library media center where she displayed photographs of favorite pets according to various categories (for example, snakes, dogs, cats, and hamsters) along with the available resources on pets.

Examples of other themes that encompass many facets include the immigrant experience (language, custom, travel, health, genealogy) and humor (pop culture, history, creative writing, comic book art, political satire). Almost any hobby, topic, or avocation can serve as the springboard for a theme appropriate for student learning.

Programs Based on
Interest and Entertainment

Although you can base a thematic program on your own expertise or experience, it may be easier and more meaningful for students if you develop programs around their interests. With entertainment as your central objective, you often have your most captive audiences at programs that explore topics that students love. Noticing what students read about or search on the Internet during their free time can provide perfect clues as to what students want to learn. From professional wrestlers, to pop music groups, to cartoon characters, there are no limits to topics based on student interest.

Variety, fun, and flexibility are the driving forces behind these programs. Programs based on interest and entertainment give you the freedom to let your imagination move to the extraordinary. These programs are especially effective when created solely for reviving student interest in the school library media center. In schools where the media center needs some good public relations (PR), a program centering on student interest can help reshape their opinions and rejuvenate their desire to frequent your facility more often.

A resurgence of student enthusiasm can do wonders for you as well. Not only can it breathe new life into your own professional creativity, but it can also motivate you to develop or repeat programs that highlight your school library media center as an inviting, lively learning environment. Best of all, learning occurs within the larger context of student pleasure. For example, by participating in a magic show sponsored by the library, the ESL students mentioned earlier sharpened their hand/eye coordination and expanded their understanding of abstract concepts of illusion without needing much verbal communication at all. Not deterred by the language barrier, the students engaged in firsthand learning.

Programs Based on
Available Time Periods

Time will always be an important factor in developing a program. The amount of time available or the time period during which the program takes place impacts the type of program you can design. Like all aspects of programming, the parameters for a time-based program are still limitless. The range may vary from a one-time 30-minute event to a program that continues and even evolves throughout the year. Commonly, short-term programs that include guest speakers may become routine parts of the school year. Special events such as a regional fall festival or the Super Bowl provide program topics on an annual basis. Programs that students may come to anticipate each year could include Teen Read Week; a fall festival; Christmas, or Kwanzaa programs in December; or a book fair in the spring.

PURPOSES OF PROGRAMS

To develop programs for middle school students and teachers, begin by specifying your purpose. At this level, most learning objectives will involve supporting and enhancing curriculum, enriching students' personal interests, or providing professional growth for teachers.

Support and Enhance the Curriculum

With few exceptions, core curriculum is the focus for all educational endeavors. Theoretically, students develop their primary thinking skills by mastering the four major subject areas: (1) language arts, (2) social studies, (3) math, and (4) science. These early stages of secondary education form the link between the more rigid adherence to standard curriculum for all students, and the more specialized tracks that students can pursue in high school.

As a result, middle school library media specialists have both the responsibility and the freedom to support the curriculum. Freedom for library media specialists has become even more empowering as today's teachers become more restricted by the national trend to make standardized tests the gauge for student achievement. Twenty years ago, public school teachers had much more creative leverage to personalize their lessons to meet particular needs of students or enhance their own unique strengths as instructors.

With an ever-increasing emphasis placed on standardized tests to determine student success, the curriculum has been strangled by test-based demands. As a result, many teachers are also restricted to sharing only pre-written lessons that they didn't create. As you know, in many districts across the country, entire teams of teachers are facing the disheartening, even stifling requirement of teaching the same lessons the same way on the same day.

Fortunately, such limitations are seldom as strictly enforced in school library media centers. In fact, advances in technology-based educational tools and the wealth of resources now available afford even greater opportunities for library media specialists to support and enhance curriculum. Through programming, you can develop original curriculum-related lessons with a flexibility of format, time, and approach seldom afforded today's teachers.

To help her begin such support, one media specialist in South Carolina updates her knowledge of the curriculum for each grade level by perusing their math, science, and social studies textbooks. She also copies the tables of contents from each textbook and files them at the front of her "program planning" drawer. When developing new programs, these resources become her first references.

English/Language Arts Curriculum

Because so many school library media specialists are former reading, English, or language arts teachers, they share a special bond with their school's English instructors. Frequently, they were working collaboratively on a teaching team long before the concept became an educational standard. English teachers naturally gravitate to school library media specialists for research material, resources, and suggestions for students who are either required to read independently, or those who enjoy recreational reading.

Your love of books and abundant access to information are a wellspring of programming ideas. Among the most effective forms of programming for English/language arts are author visits. While common at the elementary level, fewer middle school media specialists invite authors eager to visit schools and share their work with pre-teens. Works by writers such as Christopher Paul Curtis, Caroline Cooney, and Gary Paulsen resonate with middle school readers. Imagine the impact of having such writers visit a campus to share their work, writing techniques, or careers with a target audience. (See the Internet sites for "Young Adult Authors" in Chapter 6.)

Frequently, inviting an author is more costly than other types of programming. Yet middle school library media specialists often find creative ways to afford author visits. Some media specialists plan an author visit at their campus on the heels of one already scheduled at a local public library or nearby university, thereby considerably defraying the author's sometimes exorbitant speaking fee. Even if yearly author visits are not financially feasible, part of a book, travel, or contracted services budget could be reserved or transferred in anticipation of just such an event.

Like media specialists at elementary schools, you can also pool resources to divide the cost and enhance the range of an author visit. With the current push toward interlibrary loan, what better way to share resources than to also share a visit? For districts with more than one middle school, multiple campuses can gather at one location, or arrange for the author to spend parts of the day at each site. Initially unaffordable fees become manageable when you divide expenses and note the benefits to students. Sometimes, costs can be shared between your school library media center and local bookstores. Additionally, consider inviting authors who are scheduled to speak at conferences in your city. For many authors, their conference-speaking fee includes the price of their airfare and hotel. If a local organization is already paying those expenses, then your cost may be lessened considerably.

Do not dismiss the possibility of securing authors who charge little or even nothing but the chance to sell their books. Speaking engagements by lesser-known writers are often affordable. Eager to establish a positive reputation, newer writers frequently work hard to ensure that their visit is a success.

Even other English programs require little expense and no outside guest speakers. Middle school students enjoy some of the same activities frequently used at the elementary level, so long as the program is designed to meet their interests and needs. Booktalks, read alouds, or even storytelling can be very effective for the right group and topic. In one Georgia school, a library media specialist and a language arts teacher collaborated on a unit to introduce journal writing to a generally resistant group of sixth-grade boys. Between instructions and demonstrations by the teacher, the media specialist read excerpts from several My Name is America books, all written in journal format by a male protagonist. By the end of the lesson, the students grew curious about the fate of Civil War Union soldier, James Edmond Pease; Transcontinental Railroad worker, Sean Sullivan; and Finnish immigrant, Otto Peltonen. In the process, not only were they exposed to good journal-writing techniques, but were invited to reassess some limited perspectives on journal writing.

In general, poetry readings are surprisingly popular. At one school, the media specialist dedicates an entire week of poetry readings around the book, *Poetry After Lunch.* Using this anthology of read-aloud poems for middle grade and young adult readers as a springboard for original poetry writing, she invites teachers to read their favorite selections, and then share writing tips for creating poems of similar style or themes. At the end of each session, students sign up to write and share their original works the following week.

During that subsequent week, the students are the presenters, and the teachers become the audience. Without the pressure of being graded for their efforts, students are free to be more imaginative in choosing subjects and experimental in their style and diction.

Employing a similar teacher-sharing format, a colleague in my district encourages teachers to read excerpts from their favorite books to students during lunch throughout National Library Week. Not surprisingly, the range is astonishing and tremendously impressive to middle school students. In one session, students might hear *The Giver; Chamique Holdsclaw: My Story; Math Curse;* and *Yo, Alejandro.* On the last day, she invites teachers who have published poetry or prose to read from their original works, then answer questions about writing and publishing.

Because creating lifelong readers is a primary objective of all media specialists, English programs are the most frequently developed. More examples, and further details on programs like those described above, appear in Chapter 8.

Social Studies Curriculum

The diversity of social studies curriculum invites countless programming opportunities. As even the name implies, social studies lends itself to experiential interactive learning. Consequently, library media specialists frequently develop programs relating to the community, citizenship, history, culture, and geographic regions.

In schools across the country, multicultural studies have become the cornerstone of teaching tolerance and diversity. As the core of any campus, the library media center is the ideal place to offer exciting programs during multicultural week. In many cases, entire campuses host schoolwide multicultural fairs where every department is required to participate. During that week, visitors might see paper dragons cascading over the science wing during a tae kwon do demonstration, catch a whiff of tortillas wafting through the history hallway, and hear bagpipes blaring from the gym.

While no one person, even the library media specialist, should be expected to coordinate this entire festival, you should want to be on the planning committee. Beyond providing resources for teachers and students before and after the event, you could also volunteer the media center as a hub of activity. For example, it could serve as a mock United Nations, drawing together the different cultures being taught throughout the building.

Social studies curriculum also accommodates smaller programs. To incorporate geography information and help students learn about their teachers at the beginning of the year, school library media specialist Kelly Schultz posts a huge map on a bulletin board that identifies where all the teachers traveled the previous summer. Different-colored strings of yarn trace the distance from the school to each destination. Over the years, her single map has evolved into an entire display. Not only did this concept inspire more teachers to share their travel exploits, but it also prompted a faculty tradition of sending souvenir postcards to Kelly and occasionally bringing her artifacts unique to that region.

Historical places or events can also prompt programming ideas. Because her area of expertise is reading and one of her favorite genres is young adult (YA) historical fiction, a library media specialist in Illinois developed a program called "In Another Time and Place." During the multifaceted program, several activities occurred simultaneously in various parts of the room. While parent volunteers prepared specialty ethnic foods, a guest airline pilot shared a PowerPoint presentation on some of the countries he'd visited, and social studies teachers listed "Astounding Facts about Our Life in Past Decades." As a follow up to the program, the library media specialist read excerpts to students from her favorite YA historical fiction books each lunch period throughout the week of the program. Students were taken to the high seas in 1812 with *Tom Cringle: The Pirate and the Patriot,* to early twentieth-century Boston with *A Place for Joey,* and to racially divided Alabama in the 1950s with *The $66 Summer.*

This is just one example of how you can support the social studies curriculum in diverse, multifacted ways. From simple bulletin boards to events that become the common thread for an entire districtwide fair, programs on social issues, geography, or history can be fascinating learning experiences.

Science Curriculum

Science is also rife with program possibilities. Instead of being exposed to a mere overview of the different science disciplines as they are in elementary school, middle-school students can begin to delve more deeply into fields of science they might possibly study in high school. Again, as the pivotal link between these two levels of education, you as a middle-school library media specialist can facilitate more in-depth study of some of those disciplines through programming. Animals, plants, weather, astronomy, anatomy, and oceanography all contain various facets that can be explored as a single event in the school library media center. Every geographic region has resources that can stimulate dynamic program ideas.

Photo 1.1. Three-dimensional displays are one way in which seventh-graders at Neptune Middle School demonstrate their mastery of concepts from a six-week research unit. *(Neptune Middle School, Kissimmee, Florida, Osceola County Schools)*

When choosing a science topic, consider how much your school's location can inspire program topics. Coastal towns would have human and material resources for aquatic themes. Cities like Houston can capitalize on the National Aeronautics and Space Administration's (NASA's) generous offerings in the field of space exploration. Regions noted for their technology (Silicon Valley) or for agriculture (states throughout the Midwest) make logical program topics for schools in the area.

Consider also science-related industries in your region. Industries such as chemical plants, sugar factories, or textile mills would have much information to share that ties science and careers. Is your area of the country famous for some conservation efforts? Wildlife reserves, hydroponics farms, even camps that use animals to work with special needs children exist throughout the country, and can be used in programs that teach scientific concepts as well as introduce students to the diverse contributions people are making to save the earth and benefit humankind.

Finally, local weather stations of any region can provide support about climate and natural disasters. Throughout the hurricane season, weather-tracking information is available free in regions along the Atlantic Ocean and Gulf of Mexico. Tornado trackers would make fascinating guest speakers. A presentation about earthquakes can teach students much about the land, as well as unique architecture built to withstand quakes, and technological advances in machines that can predict their time, location, and intensity. Whether simple or elaborate, programs about weather safety can be profoundly useful, even life saving.

Almost any science-related idea (health and nutrition, rain forests, poison control, the ozone layer) can spark a program idea. Begin by considering the immediate region of your school, then branch out from there. The possibilities are endless.

Math Curriculum

For too long, media specialists struggled to include meaningful math resources in their collections. Bookshelves of math resources were frequently sparse and in desperate need of updating. Although new books about math may still be harder to come by than those in other core curricula, the advent of computers and a burgeoning interest in high-tech research has opened the floodgate for programs that incorporate math concepts.

Very often, special programs related to math can be offered in conjunction with some other discipline. Math classes surfing the Internet for examples of geometric shapes in architecture led one media specialist to combine science and math for a program on the topic. The media specialist and the math instructor offered a lesson on geometric shapes and buildings, reinforcing their ideas with books such as David Macaulay's *Cathedral: The Story of Its Construction* and *Castle*. The event then incorporated a science teacher who shared a lesson on unique engineering that enables buildings to withstand regional natural disasters such as earthquakes and gale-force winds. To extend the learning even further, the program's follow-up activity required students to construct their own model city, which was eventually displayed in the school library media center.

Clearly, the best programs extend beyond book learning to engage students in activities with hands-on experience. Collaborating with teachers makes the program cross-curricular, and adding unique elements inspires both excitement and creativity in your audience. While fulfilling curriculum demands, you can create a fun yet task-oriented focus that invites students to really enjoy the learning experience.

Provide Enrichment and Support
Beyond Core Curriculum

When planning programs, remember that using the media center requires skills that students must master to be effective learners. As we all know, just because students have heard the information before doesn't mean they've mastered it or even absorbed the concept. In my student teaching days at a middle school, I naively believed students who stared blankly at me and said, "We never learned that." A few weeks later, when I repeated the same information for the semester review and heard the same line, I learned an important lesson: Just because I've taught it and they learned it at the time, doesn't always mean they've retained it for the long term.

While this realization can be disheartening for classroom teachers, it sets off alarms for those of us in the library media center. If students are going to become lifelong, independent learners, it is essential that they know how to find, gather, record, and process information effectively. Re-teaching such concepts year after year can be draining. Re-teaching these concepts moment to moment for each student who comes into the library can be unbearable.

Consequently, although students theoretically know how to find books and use resources like *The Readers' Guide to Periodicals,* programs that focus on research techniques, reference books, or online databases are always worthwhile. New Internet or CD resources with unique navigation instructions make essential technology-based programs. Conversions to new computer systems require specific instructions so students can continue to pursue independent research.

Introducing students to such technology through a focused program ensures that they've at least been exposed to the information and have spent some time navigating the program themselves. Because many of these systems are designed for independent searches, introducing students to the rudiments of navigation can set them far enough on their journey to work through the rest of the system independently, or with the help of another student. If you have made clear to students what you have available, and guided them through the navigation system at least once, you have empowered them to use the resource.

Adding new search tools? Changing from hardbound resources like an encyclopedia or biographical dictionary to their online versions? Anticipating a research project where students would benefit from being shown the best places to find information? All of these make perfect program topics.

Although your patrons have frequented school library media centers since first grade, they still must learn what resources are available and how to use them. Programs on such topics keep your media center running more smoothly, while supporting curriculum in every discipline.

Fine arts electives offer myriad opportunities for programs. If you are near a big city, the local symphony, opera, or ballet company will usually be glad to send resource people and performers to schools for lectures and demonstrations. For off-campus programs, consider taking students to any of the aforementioned venues for a performance. Often for free or for a nominal cost, university drama departments have troupes that visit schools and perform everything from Shakespeare to mime. A program on music appreciation, either tightly structured to tie in with a specific learning objective or more open-ended to appeal to band, handbell choir, and keyboarding students, can be fun and educational.

Student art displayed in the school library media center can be more than decoration. Enhanced by books about great painters, displays of artists' biographies, or interactive bulletin boards where students match the painting with the artist become programs that can remain intact as long as they attract patrons. To add variety to this theme, set a date to end the display and replace it with a new one. Also, keep in mind that area university art departments may be good resources for obtaining artwork for display. For even more personal relevance to students, create displays of their work. Meet with your campus art teachers to schedule exhibits of student art throughout the school year.

Provide Personal Enrichment

Nothing breaks the archetypal misperception of libraries as being sterile, silent, and stuffy than programs generated simply for students' personal enrichment. Because you interact with all grade levels and age groups, you should probably know what interests students more than any other professional on campus. Topics that students request, books they check out consistently, and even the conversations that you interrupt to get students back on task provide clues for program topics. Also, you may distribute surveys to potential target audiences inquiring about their likes and dislikes. For program ideas, some media specialists display survey forms near a suggestion box in the school library media center.

As anyone who works with young people knows, their attention span and loyalty to a fad is often as short as a music video. Although previous generations may have seen trends shift from month to month, today's youth have a much more minute-by-minute mentality. The old adage "Here today, gone tomorrow" has never applied more literally. Generally, you can best serve yourself and your program audience by selecting a topic with lasting appeal. That way, you can update and repeat it in subsequent years. However, for target students who frequent the school library media center the least (and probably need it the most), a timely hot topic might generate interest and draw in students like no other.

Skateboarders who practice stunts over the wheelchair access ramps after school may not know about your nonfiction books like *Thrasher: The Radical Skateboard Book*. They may never have heard of Grady Grennan, the skateboarding protagonist of Randy Powell's American Library Association (ALA) Best Book winner, *Tribute to Another Dead Rock Star*. Although a standard research assignment is not likely to do more than frustrate these high-energy students, a program about extreme sports could certainly draw them in and perhaps, once they know what is available, motivate them to read.

Even though the focus of personal interest programs is usually fun, they can still be meaningful. Drama students from your district's high school are often glad to perform skits on drug and alcohol awareness and social responsibility. Though the themes are serious, the context is entertaining, and the message is usually well received because it is presented by teens.

Ordered new books on a popular topic? A simple but attractive display can draw students in and get them reading. Although you're not likely to find many middle school students who haven't read a Harry Potter book, you certainly have many who now are interested in a genre they may never have read before. Harry Potter invites several possibilities. You might create a display highlighting other YA fantasy novels, books about real castles throughout Europe, fiction works or biographies about underdogs or outsiders who do the extraordinary, books about magic and illusion, even books by authors from Edgar

Allan Poe to Lois Lowry who may have influenced Rowling's themes, style, and imagery. (For great Web sites and more programming ideas, refer to Chapter 6.)

Offering programs on topics that students are intrinsically motivated to learn more about promotes the love of reading. Motorcycles, dragons, world records, sports heroes, strange animals, pop stars, science fiction, bugs, humor and jokes, and muscle cars are among the topics you probably cover in your collection, but probably have never considered focusing on for a program. But consider all of the possibilities. If a topic brings in students who wouldn't otherwise use your media center, then you have done them a great service, and may open to them a world of learning they previously thought unreachable.

Provide Professional Development for Teachers

Few activities can make a better impression on your principal than coordinating professional growth sessions for faculty members. In some districts, it's even required. Yet what may at first seem to be another responsibility amid the endless demands of your job can be an exceptional opportunity with long-term professional benefits. These programs give you the chance to share useful information while simultaneously perpetuating a good rapport with your colleagues.

Inservice presentations can be given during specially designated inservice training days or in short snippets before or after school. In most cases, these programs will center on technology. As you've no doubt noticed over the past 10 years, teaching faculty members about new software programs and research tools has consumed nearly all inservice trainings. Yet the need is there, and you have the information, skill, and expertise to share it. Through your regular use, you have mastered many CDs, databases, and Internet search engines. You've probably used them so much that you may not realize how many teachers on campus still find technology intimidating and who couldn't even begin an independent computer search.

There may be other technology-based topics for which teachers need training that you would have no reason to use. As a school library media specialist who is (or at least should be) part of the decision-making committee on your campus, you are aware of new technology, even if it doesn't apply to your specific job. Consider this technology as a possible program topic.

Accessing lesson plans on the Internet, mastering new computerized grade books, and knowing how to incorporate multimedia presentations into classroom instruction would make useful program topics, especially for new teachers. In these cases, you might facilitate a special program while allowing someone else to teach it. On your campus, there are always other teachers, computer whizzes, or technology experts who love to share their knowledge and would appreciate the professional growth opportunity that may come in the form of monetary compensation or, more likely, administrative recognition.

As many library media specialists will testify, general inservice sessions are almost always tailored to the needs of classroom teachers. Similarly, breakout sessions not created for or by media specialists seldom contain information that applies directly to running the school library media center. Rather than spending all that time in meetings that do not support your own professional needs, why not offer an inservice on computerized resources or an online program? Because teaching a subject requires you to learn it more thoroughly, offer a program on a new resource or interactive CD you have recently purchased. You'll be an expert by the time you use it with students.

Photo 1.2. Professional development activities for teachers, like this introduction to I-books, make effective and relevant inservice presentations. *(Harry F. Byrd Middle School, Richmond, Virginia, Henrico County Public Schools)*

Hosting an inservice has several benefits. Besides providing real benefits to teachers, it also empowers them to guide students through searches when they bring classes to the school library media center. Many districts offer professional growth hours for doing inservices. Even better, some districts pay inservice instructors a small stipend or give them compensation time equal to the number of hours it takes to prepare a presentation.

And there are more benefits. A natural result of providing meaningful inservices to faculty members is good public relations for your media center. When you take an active role in helping teachers enhance their skills, you impact your colleagues and make a good impression on the administration. Just as significantly, spending extended time with teachers develops rapport. Knowing your faculty helps you identify their needs. Letting them know you makes it easier to ask for their support when developing programs in the future.

Of course, programs created for faculty members should not be limited to inservice days. Throughout the school year, you may offer a variety of mini-workshops (keep them to about 20 minutes, especially if they're offered after school when teachers are tired) on interesting topics. These sessions will probably not count toward inservice credit, but they will reap many of the same benefits of supporting your colleagues, enhancing your reputation, and promoting your media center.

To develop such programs, begin by asking faculty members what topics they would enjoy or what they need to enhance their effectiveness in the classroom.

Suggested Topics for Faculty

- Relaxation techniques that lower stress and improve health
- Dress for success (on a teacher's budget)
- Classroom arrangements for all learning styles
- New computer programs
- Navigating online resources (for example, *S.I.R.S.*, *Newsbank*)
- Introduction to grant writing
- New reference resources available in the school library media center
- The best YA author Web sites
- Customize TV game shows for test reviews
- Self-esteem building exercises you can model for students.

In addition to this list of topics, you can find related Web sites listed in Chapter 6 and detailed programs for faculty described in Chapter 8.

BENEFITS OF PROGRAMMING

Incorporating special programs into your daily routine promises many benefits and rewards. They give you the opportunity to highlight your school library media center as well as your staff or volunteers. At the same time, programming increases use of the school library media center, provides classroom support, broadens personal interests, generates outstanding PR opportunities for you, and most important of all, encourages the development of lifelong learners.

Programs Highlight the
School Library Media Center

After attending a program, students and faculty members get a much richer sense of the diverse, multidimensional world you coordinate every day as a school library media specialist. By visiting during a well-structured, meaningful, and enjoyable event, they become more comfortable in the environment and understand more fully all that the school library media center has to offer. Seeing attractive displays, unique learning centers, and diverse hard copy and electronic resources is both inviting and stimulating, even to high-energy young people like middle-school students.

Programs Highlight the
School Library Media Specialist

Although they may never appreciate all the behind-the-scenes responsibilities required to run a library media center, students, teachers, and administrators do get a first-hand look at the fruits of your labor. Besides recognizing the varied knowledge you have in many disciplines, your colleagues come to appreciate that your commitment to students and your creative contribution to their learning is the closest and probably the strongest professional support they have.

Through programs, students develop a better appreciation for the library media specialist as well. Instead of being only that voice who reminds students ad nauseam to log off their program before leaving the computer, or not to bring food or gum into the media center, you can instead be recognized as the host of that great event, or the person who recommended those new titles that got them reading or helped them through a challenging assignment.

Programs Highlight the
School Library Media Staff

Programs also give your staff members or volunteers meaningful tasks that have direct relevance to students. How rewarding it would be for volunteers to interact with students for a day, even if only directing them to and from a presentation area, instead of filing for hours, or entering data in a computer alone each day. In the process, students and faculty members get to interact with them, see the people who periodically support your efforts, and discover which parents or local community members give their time and energy to the school.

Programs Increase
School Library Media Center Usage

To make their day both meaningful and enjoyable, students need good teachers, and this term includes library media specialists, who inspire them by sharing solid content in an engaging context. In the school library media center, that combination is best achieved through programming.

Strong programs bring students into the media center and often motivate them to return. Because all programs should include a selection of resources for further study, book circulation increases. Even those students who don't become regular patrons will at some point need to step back in to return a book they checked out. At that time, they may be drawn to an interest center or display that piques their curiosity.

Increased book circulation and patron usage also serve you financially. When you plan the following year's budget or request extra money for unique needs that inevitably arise, impressive circulation records and a well-frequented center are useful persuasion tools for convincing your principal to grant financial requests.

Programs Support and Enrich
Classroom Learning

Nearly every activity in the library media center enhances classwork. Whether your program serves as a springboard for an upcoming class unit, or, as is more often the case, as reinforcement following a classroom lesson, programs support and enrich classroom learning. Sometimes programs can complete a concept that couldn't be covered sufficiently in the classroom. With curriculum demands continually increasing, teachers are often forced to move on to a new unit to at least introduce every concept specified in the curriculum. In many cases, you can create programs that re-teach or share from a different perspective a concept that students have not successfully grasped the first time.

Even indirect support can be effective. Offering a brief presentation on a hard-to-find topic can provide invaluable support to classroom learning. For Black History Month, one teacher assigned African-American author biographies, but focused on writers from the past. Because resources on those authors were scarce, the media specialist developed a special program on those writers, sharing their poetry, excerpts from their prose, and biographical information on those authors who were difficult to find in reference books and on the Internet.

Often, doing a program on a course recently added to the curriculum can help generate interest in the class. Because instructors selected to teach the course might be tackling new curriculum themselves, collaborating with the instructors to present a program can help them clarify their course goals and help you decide what resources to order. Inevitably, the goal clarification and new resources enhance student learning.

Providing enrichment for classroom learning has many rewards. Media specialists who collaborate with teachers gain their support with increased patronage, better feedback when requesting input for purchasing new resources, and a generally more cooperative attitude when teachers bring students in for research. By making their job easier and more effective, you often inspire them to repay the courtesy.

Programs Broaden Student
and Teacher Interest

Students with a passion for any subject will gladly research it again and again. Perhaps it is a symptom of growing up in the cable television age where they may see the same show or movie rerun countless times in any given week, but middle school students today seem comfortable with the same kind of repetition enjoyed by preschoolers who are first learning new concepts.

Yet there is so much for students to discover in the all-too-brief middle school years. All they have yet to learn becomes the perfect garden where new program ideas can grow. To find a program topic, brainstorm ideas beginning with a current student interest and keep "linking" to new possibilities until the ideal program topic materializes. Like site links on the Internet, students interested in the Galveston hurricane of 1900 could be introduced to information on different hurricanes throughout the twentieth century, which could lead them to facts about other types of storms, which could in turn teach them about the weather in general.

The same principle can work for teachers. Often, new teachers participate in ice-breaker activities at their first inservices to help them get acquainted with their new co-workers. After that, many teachers find a narrow niche and interact solely with their own grade-level team, other teachers in their department, or those few teachers at their end of the hall with the same conference period. Programs directed at broadening teacher interest can do much for campus morale. Isolated in their classrooms and constantly inundated with new state and district demands, many teachers would relish knowing that their heavy load is being shared by a colleague with inventive approaches that add depth and dimension to student learning.

Interested in offering some personal affirmations to teachers? Surveying them about their personal hobbies can inspire program ideas. Discover what they enjoy and find volunteers who would like to share their talents during a brief program for students. If their hobby results in a finished product, such as woodcarvings, tufted pictures, or patchwork quilts, display their work along with arts and crafts or other related books and a brief biography of the teacher. Such simple touches can profoundly encourage independent learning and give teachers a boost of recognition that may otherwise go unexpressed.

Have some faculty members won unique awards or do they have unusual collections? Locked display cases are ideal for sharing teachers' achievements or collections. Scanned copies of a stamp collection could tie in meaningfully with a history lesson on the subjects depicted on the stamps or the time period when they were first printed. Although not everyone wants to share original collections with even the most trustworthy library media specialist, others relish the opportunity to discuss their hobbies and teach students how to begin a collection of their own.

While affirming colleagues and teaching new concepts to patrons, such programs cement your professional relationships with teachers. Personalizing connections between colleagues benefits both members professionally, and sets an example for students about the importance of respecting co-workers and honoring their unique contributions.

Programs Enhance Public Relations

Special events generate great PR. In addition to consistently supporting staff and helping students establish a good rapport with patrons, programs also make strong impressions.

Through programs, you help dispel any negative perceptions that students might have of their school library media center. Even students who enjoy reading may view the media center as a mere book repository or place where rigidity and silence are the order of the day. Vibrant programs enliven your facility. Attractive displays, interesting centers, and new, varied resources transform a drab setting into a stimulating learning environment.

Although revitalizing the physical surroundings may ignite a spark of interest in students, teachers will more quickly value the content of your contributions. Whether a multifaceted event where several learning opportunities are transpiring simultaneously, or even a simple interactive bulletin board that introduces one teacher's upcoming unit, programs make your facility the center of positive activity. A dreary environment is an invitation for restless students to stir up some excitement. With programs, you create the excitement and invite students to join you in unique learning experiences.

**Photo 1.3. Principal Larry Larson and Assistant Principal Mary Thompson
encourage lifelong learning by participating in a
schoolwide reading incentive program.**
(Rosemount Middle School, Rosemount, Minnesota Independent School District 196)

Programs Inspire Lifelong Learning

A primary goal of all educators is to develop lifelong readers and learners. By providing positive experiences with books and creating educational activities that stimulate curiosity, you allow students to recognize the joy of learning. Vibrant, fun, yet educationally sound events make school library media centers come alive. They revitalize a drab facility, enervate the media specialist, and at their best, motivate students to read. For a generation whose brains are conditioned for multi-image, click-and-go stimuli, it's no wonder some see a book as nothing more than a doorstop.

Although we need not host multimedia extravaganzas just to get a book in students' hands, we do need to reach them in ways that are meaningful. Simply recommending a good book to some students may not inspire a lifelong interest in reading. But, if you draw students to books through programs that pique their curiosity or challenge their intellect, you may well set them on a path of independent learning that can serve them for a lifetime.

CONCLUSION

Nearly all of our day-to-day responsibilities as library media specialists require us to focus on the educational development of students. But to really reach them, we must put students center stage, and create activities that immerse them in challenging, exciting, and motivating experiences. Those experiences are best presented as programs.

There are many ways to begin the process of creating and developing a program. Determine a topic or theme that you know will interest students. Consider the various formats that provide a creative outlet for teaching a new concept. Think of different audiences who could benefit from a program. Whatever ideas inspire you, embrace them, nurture them, and let them grow. If your experience is anything like ours, one spark may help you discover the impact of programming and the value it offers for you, your students, and your entire school.

2

Initial Stages of Program Planning

T he stages of programming can most generally be defined as preparation, execution, and assessment. No matter what your budget, or program theme, each stage involves clear, workable tasks that ensure program success. Through experience, of course, you will find unique approaches or modifications to the planning template. What works best or is most effective in one school or district may not fit your vision or most effectively meet the needs of your target population. Nevertheless, adhering to these standards of detailed planning, following the protocol that emphasizes consideration of others, and capitalizing on some convenient shortcuts shared by our school library media specialists who are highlighted in Chapter 8 will maximize the success of any program, even your first.

As library media specialists, we almost all instinctively recognize the unique needs of our student population and begin developing a plan to meet them. In the process, we often discover that the good works we do for one group create a ripple effect, enhancing the learning experience for students in general, and impressing upon faculty members and administration the integral role of the library media center in the school. To begin any project with such far-reaching goals in mind would be overwhelming. Yet targeting a specific group and meeting their learning needs in a context that the entire school recognizes as valuable sets into motion just such a ripple effect. That context, of course, is programming.

Interestingly, when we surveyed library media specialists for the first book in this series, many responded apologetically, "I don't do programming." Yet further descriptions of their activities revealed an eye-opening truth: Most of us do programming without knowing it. Until this Library Programs That Inspire series, we media specialists had no current resources to define programming or to show us the steps for putting a program together or assessing it. Consequently, we continued to work from instinct, using our experience as teachers and media specialists to develop and refine events that might spark interest in our patrons. We thought of them as lessons, special events, activities, or cooperative teaching strategies, almost anything but programs. Without the parameters that define and unify this specific teaching approach, we media specialists often ventured out on our own, feeling the exhilaration of doing something worthwhile for students, but also experiencing the isolation that comes from believing that we're treading new ground.

No more. With any book in this resource series, we library media specialists can identify our unique events as programs. Better still, we can see their universal benefits. They draw patrons into our library media centers. They impress upon students how much our library media centers have to offer each of them. They invite cooperative teaching opportunities that strengthen lessons and confirm our central role in the education of all students in our schools. They help us establish a positive rapport with our colleagues. They enable us to show the students, faculty members, our administration, and the community the value of what we do and what a school library media center can be when used to its fullest capacity. And finally, it gives us an effective, increasingly recognized educational venue for using our creative energy to its greatest potential.

To illustrate the stages of program development, Holly Blaylock, library media specialist at Killough Middle School in Houston's Alief Independent School District, provides a thorough example of how she prepared, executed, and assessed one of her many successful programs. The italicized scenario, shared incrementally through Chapters 2, 3, and 7, traces the entire process of a single, multifaceted program, and serves as a general template for the stages of library programming that can be adapted to fit your patrons' needs and your personal style.

GATHERING IDEAS
TO DETERMINE A THEME

Killough Middle School's library media center serves 1,150 students. During my first year as library media specialist, I maintained the same schedule and routines set up by my predecessor. Although the media center was a vital part of the school, I realized that I could do even more to bring my facility and its services to the forefront of the school community. I wanted to expose students and staff to speakers, authors, musicians, and displays of various interests.

The following year, I read about three outstanding speakers: Christopher Paul Curtis, David Wisniewski, and a storyteller from Dallas, Katherine Whiteman. After I saw what three professionals could do when brought in to share their talents with students, I was inspired to coordinate an event myself. After mulling over several possibilities, my program was literally laid right on my desk. While trying to think of a way to develop an original evening program to promote our yearly book fair, I saw on my desk a flyer about a mid-year concert by some of our fine arts classes.

That's it! I thought. I could extend my book fair into a program that included some of our fine arts students to which we could also invite parents to visit the school in a positive setting.

Choosing a topic is the first and most defining step in the preparation phase of programming. Although selecting a topic carries no concrete requirements, there are five factors that result in the best topic choice:

1. It should interest your target audience. (The most common audiences are students, faculty members, and parents.)

2. It should have educational merit for your target audience. (The educational element can be extracurricular.)

3. It should be a topic that you are genuinely enthusiastic about sharing. (Because you will spend extensive time working on the program, you want to enjoy the process.)

4. It should be a relatively easy topic to develop. (Choose a topic about which you can easily find information and that has a plethora of resources you can access.)

5. It should be a topic that you can share effectively in whatever setting you choose. (Although you will usually present programs in your library media center, examples throughout this text will suggest other unique places—a classroom or computer lab, school parking lot, even off-campus locations—that can serve as program sites.)

Ideas for program topics exist everywhere. Simply observing potential target audiences or considering ideas independently can generate abundant possibilities. However, brainstorming with teachers, students, and other media specialists is usually faster and more productive. If you choose a target audience first, then it will immediately become apparent with whom you can brainstorm. For example, if you want to develop a program for a seventh-grade social studies class, then brainstorming with those grade-level teachers, that subject-area team, and even those students can help you identify immediately what your target audience likes, needs, and would respond to.

Although curriculum-based programs are important, programs that solely address student interests or more aesthetic pursuits are equally worthwhile. Thus, if you begin by choosing a program purpose first, then your initial planning may follow a different path. Inspired by a character-building campaign initiated by her principal, a media specialist in Kentucky decided to develop a program around the concept of good manners. Beginning with her purpose of teaching concrete etiquette skills, she set out to determine an audience, a format, and a setting. The result was a dinner party attended by her target group of upcoming National Honor Society candidates. For the event, the group of 20 students created formal, computer-generated invitations, learned the dining etiquette rules of different cultures, demonstrated a mastery of those rules at the media specialist's dinner party held in the adjoining high school's home economics classroom, and then wrote personalized thank-you notes. Though the process was simple and the context recreational, the learning was specific and valuable.

Some media specialists stumble upon program topics unexpectedly. Occasionally, a particular timely issue piques students' interest, and current information is abundant. Whenever hurricanes or tropical storms hit, they generate so much press that media specialists can gather enough information to develop bulletin boards, displays, even entire program events supplemented by articles and video footage.

When considering program ideas, keep in mind teachers' interests and needs as well. If you know of specific hobbies about which some teachers are passionate, consider asking them to share resources, offer insights, or even present at a special program tailored to their area of expertise. At other times, you might note teachers' specific needs and plan something to support them. That support can be professional or personal. Rather than simply ordering resources for a new unit or discipline, invite vendors who carry related material to present their newest resources on the topic, and let the teachers decide which they think will best meet their curricular needs. On a personal level, you can also support teachers through programming.

In one district in Colorado, a middle-school media specialist heard that a nearby high school had a massage therapist visit their campus once a week to give 15-minute back rubs to teachers who signed up and paid the nominal fee of $10.00. Although the middle school could not arrange the same plan, the media specialist developed a one-day program around her theme, "Past Tense." Throughout the day, teachers could visit the school library media center where the school nurse taught relaxation techniques, a yoga instructor demonstrated de-stressing stretching exercises, and a local physician spoke about the warning signs of stress-induced conditions and provided handouts on nutrition and exercise regimens that promote better health. Even more valuable to teachers than the information was realizing to what lengths their school library media specialist would go to help enhance their well-being.

No matter what topic you select, take the advice I give my students when they begin a writing assignment: If you're not interested in it, no one else will be either. Select a program topic because you are passionate about the subject, because you see its value, or because you are eager (or at least willing) to learn more about it yourself.

Informal Observation

Once you find a topic that piques your interest, see if it has potential for a target audience. Begin by making informal observations.

You can discover program topics in many places. While conversing with teachers, listen for their curriculum needs. Search your vertical files for ideas. Go through your file cabinets and look for past units on which you've collaborated with teachers. Examine course textbooks. Skim curriculum guides to refresh your memory of what skills and concepts teachers must cover. Finally, ask the administrator in charge of curriculum for practice tests or review sheets for standardized tests. Seeing what students must know can inspire many potential program topics.

As you prepare lessons with teachers who will bring their students in for research, watch for program ideas that spark enthusiasm. Casual conversations with colleagues may also lead to idea development. Interacting with staff over lunch will help you narrow your options. Most important, attending school meetings of all sorts will keep you in touch with school goals, student needs, and district plans. Besides attending general faculty meetings, ask to sit in on meetings of the more specialized groups on campus. Department or grade-level meetings reveal volumes about the strengths and needs within each discipline. Because it would be unrealistic to try to attend all meetings, be selective. With focus and attention, you can acquire many significant ideas from a single meeting.

Also consider joining committees whose work affects the school. If your school has one, the Site-Based Decision-Making Committee (often known simply as the SBDMC) on your campus is probably every bit as influential as the administrative staff. If the responsibilities of that committee seem too heavy considering all your other duties, volunteer to be on the social committee. Members are almost always outgoing, and the emphasis of their work is fun.

Other Media Specialists' Expertise

For several weeks I discussed with my library paraprofessional, Robin, the idea of transforming our usual book fair into an entire program that included performances by our fine arts students. We talked about all the possibilities that a night like this could provide for our school. Our dialogue extended to some teachers who are friendly patrons of the school library media center. That's when the idea, and the excitement, started to grow.

Even though you may only meet with them once a month, or even just during district-wide faculty inservice days, other media specialists may be your best resources outside your campus. Their shared experiences give you not only common goals, but also access to expertise in all facets of the job, including programming. In most districts, other media specialists generously share resources that can enhance programming. As you do with teachers, brainstorm with other media specialists. They can offer a wealth of information, including everything from strange glitches in your district's budgeting procedures for special events to knowing which local businesses underwrite program costs or provide volunteer presenters.

Best of all, many will have firsthand experience with local guest speakers and visiting authors. Such brainstorming sessions may also result in collaborative programs. If an author visit is too expensive for one school to host, it may become more affordable when several campuses pool their resources. A multiple-campus program allows you and your colleagues to share workloads, responsibilities, and credit for an event large enough to warrant attention from district administration and perhaps even the local media.

If you never offer combined programs, you and your local library media specialist colleagues can still work cooperatively. The computerized interlibrary loan systems now used by many districts make acquiring resources even easier. Even if your district doesn't subscribe to one, your media center colleagues can still provide extra materials for putting together a program, or books to circulate as follow-up support to the program.

Faculty Suggestions

In October, I presented this idea to our school leadership team that consisted of the principal, three assistant principals, three counselors, a language arts specialist, math specialist, technology specialist, and me. Our team meets weekly throughout the year and provides an opportunity to discuss plans for the school. The team members all responded positively to my program idea of having an evening event to showcase our students' talents and provide parents the opportunity to visit the school during the book fair.

Some committee members pointed out that this type of program would benefit faculty and students. During the always-hectic month of December, each performing arts class (choir, band, orchestra, handbells) gives an individual concert. With this event, we could combine all performances into one evening. Thus, teachers needed to come to school only one evening to support their students.

Because we have students of all socioeconomic backgrounds and various academic levels, this event could combine the arts with the more academic book fair to create a positive, inviting atmosphere for all students and their parents.

Even if you aren't able to participate in their small group meetings, it's always beneficial to solicit input from teachers. Your partnership with them is essential, and it requires consistent, meaningful communication. If you are included in the weekly department chairperson meetings, listen to teacher concerns and note new philosophical directions in which the district seems to be moving. Ask teachers what units they find particularly challenging. Many times a few open-ended questions can reveal untapped program ideas with great potential. Throughout this stage, you need not explain why you are gathering ideas. Just casually inquire, and then keep a file of notes for future reference.

If a faculty member suggests a promising program topic, first check to see what resources you already have. In subsequent meetings, if the idea still seems worthwhile, brainstorm the possibilities further. During that session, discover what other resources that teacher has and what contacts might have some as well. Pinpoint as many concrete ideas as possible and continue the dialogue until the initial suggestion takes shape as a workable, effective program concept. Pursued thoroughly, a single brainstorming session often provides the information from which your entire program can be developed. As important, that single meeting will likely introduce other program ideas that can be explored later.

Eventually, you may discover that a formal survey is in order. From that feedback you may see multiple ideas materializing into one program topic. Your approach to acquiring this information will determine the value and volume of responses. Rather than simply asking for feedback (which most teachers perceive as just more paperwork), you may use the following contest in Figure 2.1, which gives your colleagues a special incentive to give you the feedback you want.

WANTED: PROGRAM SUGGESTIONS

Would you like to determine how $500 of the school library media center book budget gets spent? Do you have a favorite author you want students to read? How about a hobby you'd like covered more thoroughly in our media center? Just give me your feedback and you're eligible to have those dream resources at your disposal. If your survey responses inspire my next program, I will order the resources you list at the end of the survey, and reserve them for you first immediately after they arrive. Give five responses; determine $500 worth of new resources. What a bargain!

My students could use more information on

_____

_____

_____

I would be interested in seeing a program about

_____

_____

_____

A new topic or objective we are covering this year is

_____

_____

_____

If my students could learn only one thing, it would be

_____

_____

_____

If my suggestions inspire the next program, I would like you to order the following re-sources (you may highlight titles from catalogs, or list topics and I'll search for books for you):

_____

_____

_____

_____

_____

_____

_____

_____

_____

Figure 2.1 Faculty suggestion survey.

Student Interests

Pay attention continuously to the topics students research for personal interest and what issues they talk about among themselves. Even if some ideas initially seem basic and unoriginal to you, remember that some common areas of interest, such as sporting events or the traditions of some school clubs, are new experiences for most students. If you can muster enthusiasm for what seem to be predictable student interests, then you may create a program that can be repeated for many years.

Consider program themes that cover current fads or topics with more lasting appeal. Some topics such as UFOs, ESP, and even celebrities like Selena and Princess Diana, continue to intrigue middle school students. Conversely, some student interests shift rapidly. The cutting edge is sharp, but it is also narrow. Therefore, if you pick a trendy topic, offer the program in a timely manner. If you hear that a specific interest is hot at Christmas, you may be surprised to discover how quickly students have cooled to it by spring break. However, never underestimate the power of "the hot trend of the day." If you have students that you're especially eager to reach, a program on their favorite hot topic might ignite a spark when nothing else will.

As with teachers, surveying students is an excellent way to discover what they like and what they want to know more about. Surveys like the example in Figure 2.2 can be given to homeroom or first-period teachers to distribute and collect at the beginning of the school year. If this seems too obtrusive, consider including this survey as part of any orientations you offer, or even work it into blocks of time when teachers bring in students for study or research. No matter how you initially share the survey, leave a stack of survey sheets beside a suggestion box in a prominent place in your school library media center. Not surprisingly, your regular patrons will often be most enthusiastic and consistent about giving you honest feedback on the survey form.

Finally, if you pick a topic that is popular with young people but relatively new to you, let a few dependable students who love the topic help plan and execute the program. There are several benefits. Often they are thrilled to work on the program, and their enthusiasm is contagious. Their word-of-mouth promotions will draw program participants you may not reach otherwise. And they will help with accuracy. Knowing the lexicon of any area of interest is essential to establishing credibility. Just as we are sensitive to gender bias and errant or unsubstantiated assertions in books we order, young people can immediately spot a presenter who has learned their information from textbooks without personalizing the lesson with the appropriate lexicon of those most interested in the topic. A simple but significant example comes from one of my co-author's experiences. When preparing a program on rap music, he was abruptly corrected by a student aide for saying "rap singer" instead of the correct term, "rapper." Had he made that error during the program presentation, he would have lost credibility immediately with his audience.

STUDENT INTEREST SURVEY

Grade: _____   Sex: M _____ F _____

What are some of your favorite books?

_____
_____
_____

Who are your favorite authors?

_____
_____
_____

What hobbies, sports, and pastimes do you enjoy?

_____
_____
_____

What types of books do you enjoy reading?

Fiction	Nonfiction
_____ Realistic Fiction	_____ General Information
_____ Mystery	_____ Self Help/Inspiration
_____ Science Fiction	_____ Sports/Recreation
_____ Fantasy	_____ Biography/True Adventure
_____ Romance	_____ Social Issues
_____ Horror	_____ History
_____ Poetry	_____ Religion/Mythology
_____ Other (list below)	_____ Other (list below)

_____   _____
_____   _____
_____   _____

What subject areas interest you as program topics?
(Rank your top 3 choices, 1 being your favorite.)

_____ Computers	_____ Science
_____ Inspiration/Motivation	_____ Health and Fitness
_____ Religions of the World	_____ The Arts/ Entertainment
_____ Political and Social Issues	_____ Literature/Authors
_____ Foreign Languages/Cultures	_____ History/Biography

_____ Others topics (please list) _____
_____

Figure 2.2 Student interest survey.

Curriculum Needs

Matching program topics with course learning objectives requires knowing the curriculum. Although working with teachers familiarizes you with many class units and subject-area goals, a more precise familiarity with the curriculum can open other program possibilities. Begin by perusing subject-area textbooks and curriculum guides, which contain the core information about each subject at every grade level. Knowing the scope and sequence—what topics are covered and when—can also prove valuable. Finally, your own experience working with different teachers tells you who the experts are on each unit. Securing their support and assistance for programs covering topics they've mastered can add considerably to the depth and breadth of your program.

Familiarity with the curriculum also comes from serving on curriculum committees and attending grade-level meetings. Many administrators already appreciate the need to have you on such committees, and they include you as part of the top decision-making team. Others may have to be reminded how important you are to the school. Your extensive knowledge of existing policies and curriculum makes a credible argument for inclusion. Also, sharing information about the outstanding resources in your media center reminds your administrators how invaluable you are to the success of your school.

If your principal does not see the need for you to become actively involved, be forthright, be persuasive, and be insistent if you must, but become part of the school's decision-making team. The meetings will provide relevant information about curriculum needs and classroom activities. They are also the perfect forums for generating program ideas. In the end, everyone benefits from the collaborative effort. The curriculum is enriched and supported, brainstorming sessions are more fruitful, resource circulation increases, and student learning is enhanced.

Professional Development Activities

Attending conferences, workshops, and courses in your school district and at universities can enhance program development. With your sights focused on finding ideas or special topics at such events, you will quickly discover that program topics appear everywhere. Also, professional journals and teacher magazines are excellent sources for event ideas. Reading about programs that worked for someone else (such as those in Chapter 8) may motivate you to design a similar program or develop a more elaborate one on the same topic. Finally, perusing professional collections at the district or campus level can suggest program themes and reveal more resources, too.

Community Happenings

Local events trigger program ideas. Every community participates in special holidays, festivals, fairs, or cultural activities that can suggest topics for school library media center programs. Even better, many community organizations, universities, bookstores, and museums often host their own special programs that can trigger your program ideas and provide resources. Tying in your program to the community event is a great way to enhance both. To do so, you must know the dates and speakers involved in such activities. Outstanding programs can result from all types of local events, such as the Strawberry Festival in Pasadena, Texas, or a hot-air balloon extravaganza in Albuquerque, New Mexico.

That very event inspired one perceptive media specialist to imagine how well the local "Balloon Fest" could translate into a fun-filled school library media center program. Beyond just observing and teaching about hot-air balloons exclusively, she broadened her topic to include a history lesson on both the technological evolution of aviation and transportation, and a science lesson on gravity and gases. Clearly, ideas, approaches, and formats for any subject are endless.

Besides events, special holidays make excellent program topics. Bored with the usual Thanksgiving, Christmas, and Valentine themes? Use programs to help students learn about elections or veterans in November, Martin Luther King, Jr. in January, and Mexico's traditions and history on Cinco de Mayo.

Seeking topics with more immediacy for students? Check out upcoming local events. Find out when they are going to occur and who is involved. Such information can spark program ideas and potential sources for supporting materials. Ideas also abound in local newspapers and magazines, and on radio and television. If you prefer a more direct approach, call the local Chamber of Commerce and request the community calendar of events, or contact the community events coordinator. You may carry over some events to your library media center.

Community resources encompass many kinds of events and support. They include special events, people, places, and things that can help you determine themes and plan your program. Chapters 4 and 5 list various types of community resources for generating program ideas. Chapter 6 provides Internet sites for the community resources.

DEVELOPING A SPECIFIC PLAN

A good plan of action can immediately set you on course toward a successful program. First, formulate precise program goals. Define them clearly and pursue them systematically. Keep the scope of your program manageable by targeting only the most important goals and specifying exactly who your program audience will be. Then gather resources. Collecting materials at your immediate disposal will spark further program ideas and other potential resource providers. In the first planning phase, you may generate many more ideas and materials than you need. By phase two of program planning, where you develop and narrow your theme, you can weed out the excess.

To mold general ideas into a concrete, workable plan, answer the following questions:

- What are my general goals for the program?
- Who will this topic interest (grade, age, gender)?
- What format (displays, centers, speakers) will I use for this program?
- Where will I find available resources on the topic?
- When is the best date and time to offer the program?
- What are the logistics for carrying out this program?

Setting Goals

Thanks to brainstorming sessions with my paraprofessional colleague, Robin, and suggestions from faculty members, I had clear enough direction for my program plans to formulate specific goals that I wanted my program to achieve. After some refining, I made these my program goals:

- Provide an opportunity for students to perform or display their artistic work (band, choir, orchestra, handbells, art, dance, and poetry)
- Build school and community spirit
- Provide an opportunity for students and families to attend the school book fair
- Provide recruiting opportunities for fine arts programs in our school
- Provide opportunities for students to practice proper audience and performance etiquette
- Improve school profits from book fair

Once you've established a theme and outlined your general program ideas, you can develop concrete program goals. Begin with the end in mind. List the precise purposes for the program. What final results will participants derive from the program? In developing the goals, relate every one either to curriculum or to the personal interests of students and faculty members. Programs based on such goals are unquestionably relevant to participants. If it helps solidify your plans, write the goals in lesson-plan format to get a structured planning process and specify clear learning objectives.

Even though you want to keep your goals clear and straightforward, realize that some of the best programs use a combination of approaches.

Considering the Audience

I selected staff as my target audience, and students and their families. The last group was especially important because I wanted parents and younger siblings to see the exciting programs offered at the middle school level and to participate in and support the book fair.

When developing programs for students, match the theme to the age, interests, and gender of the audience. In middle school especially, also consider such factors as the maturity level of students and the best presentation formats for your potential audience. Rarely, you may plan a program for all students in the school, but such programs should be tackled by a committee of people rather than just one person. Schoolwide multicultural fairs or heritage festivals may include enough varied activities and learning objectives to benefit all students, but the best programs are usually more precisely targeted to meet specific learning objectives for one group. Naturally, the learning objectives and activities for an eighth grader in the gifted and talented or honors program would be vastly different from those meant for a sixth-grade life-skills or even at-risk populations.

Limiting your audience to a specific group lets you fulfill their learning needs more directly. Also, events for smaller populations are easier to schedule. It would be unrealistic to plan huge extravaganzas regularly. But, you could potentially offer programs monthly by planning small group events or choosing simple program ideas like those shared in Chapter 8.

Matching the appropriate audience to the topic is essential. After specifying your topic and planning your program activities, ask yourself the following questions:

- Is my topic appropriate for my audience?

- Will the topic pique the audience's interest?

- Are the length and content of the activities appropriate for the audience's maturity level?

- Will the planned activities hold their attention?

- What prior knowledge must my audience have to participate fully in the program?

- What new knowledge will they gain from it?

Your target audience can also be faculty members or parents. Programs for faculty members (some are also shared in Chapter 8) may cover professional growth topics ranging from technology to reference materials to young adult literature. During a faculty workshop titled "What They're Reading," a media specialist in Wisconsin presented booktalks on the most frequently circulated books in her collection. Her 20-minute program familiarized teachers with her collection and informed them about students' personal interests.

As a book reviewer for the American Library Association's *Booklist*, my co-author has hosted programs on book reviewing. Whether as an inservice presentation to help colleagues with collection development, or as a tool to help parents or teachers select resources appropriate for teens, this kind of program is consistently popular and effective.

Although parents are frequently asked to volunteer to work at programs or events, they are seldom invited as guests. Yet what an enthusiastic, appreciative audience they often make. Programs hosted for parents can provide information concerning their children, or be directly tailored to their own needs. With the counseling team, you might offer a program informing parents about new classes their children may take, new standardized test requirements that count toward promotion, different opportunities for vocational education being introduced now even in middle school curriculum. If you'd like to host a program more personally beneficial to parents, you might offer something relating to the past, present, or future.

During your district's homecoming week, you might create a nostalgic program centering on the decade in which most of the parents grew up. Around Mother's Day, one library media specialist in Oregon traditionally invites the mothers of all her student volunteers to a special appreciation luncheon that includes a slide show created by her students and appreciation speeches by them as well. After Christmas break, you might offer a program on goal setting or healthy weight loss regimens. In the spring, invite an accountant to share tax tips. Reaching out to the community not only gives you a welcome break from your routine, but it also generates outstanding PR for your library media center and school.

Determining a Time Frame

Early in the planning process, determine a time frame for your event. Other factors will often dictate the length of your program. Some time frames are predetermined because of your audience. If you offer a program to faculty members during the school day, it must be short so they can attend on their conference period.

Program format can also determine a time frame. Video presentations, for example, last as long as the segment you choose to show. Demonstrations last as long as it takes the presenter to share a process. Guest speakers may determine how long they can stay, or how much information or expertise they have to share. Displays and exhibits may not require a set time, but may simply be available for students to view or interact with whenever they choose. Most often, program time frames are set by the school-bell schedule. Except for special programs that you schedule like field trips and pull students from their regular classes, confine programs to single class periods, factoring in the time it takes for students to arrive and settle down.

Identifying Resources

For this program, students and teachers were my primary resources for the event. In addition, I created displays in the school library media center. Our theme for these displays was "Reading in a Winter Wonderland" which featured both fiction and nonfiction books. Among the books we displayed were "What Child is This?" by Caroline Cooney, "Christmas in Heaven" by Carol Lynch Williams, "The Christmas Adventure of Space Elf Sam" by Audrey Wood, "A Christmas Carol" by Charles Dickens, "A Newbery Christmas: Fourteen Stories of Christmas" by Newbery award-winning authors, and numerous nonfiction books about winter festivals around the world.

Once you've clarified your program goals, target audience, and specific program time frame, you can identify what materials you'll need. To select resources, consider the following:

- age of audience

- maturity level of audience

- interest level of audience

- audience's background knowledge of topic

- content of material

- appropriateness of material for a school program

- appropriateness of material for program format

- currency of resources

- accessibility of resources

- availability of supporting resources on topic

When identifying program resources, consider what you already have in your own facility, what your colleagues in other school library media centers in your district might share, and, if you belong to a regional or state library loan organization, what you may borrow from participating campuses. Also realize that the region where you work has unique industries and attractions with potentially outstanding materials they lend to schools at no charge or for a nominal fee. For example, resources for a program about the rodeo are plentiful in Houston, which sponsors one of the largest livestock shows and rodeos in the world. Similarly, motion picture resources would be more accessible to schools in southern California, and equipment for aquatic themes could be found in either tropical areas or along any coast where fishing and sailing are major interests. Therefore, keep in mind that each geographic region contains abundant resources that can make static presentations come alive with hands-on access to materials.

Many types of resources can support programming. Media software, young adult literature, professional books, exhibits, and displays are among the most frequently used resources. Additionally, teacher-made and student-generated resources are readily available to enrich media center programs. Because this topic includes so much information, Chapter 4 is devoted to identifying and locating resources.

Choosing a Format

After you've gathered or accessed your resources, you will have a much clearer sense of how much time you have to prepare and execute your program. Determining a format at this stage is important because format often dictates preparation time and program length. Programs range from simple displays to sophisticated full-day or ongoing events. Some of the most manageable and effective program formats are described below. As you consider them, note what variety you have in choosing a program format. Programs of any type can be as simple or as elaborate as you desire. To select your format, consider time, audience, facility space, and established goals. Simple programs usually require only a single format. Elaborate events often incorporate several formats to vary activities and meet multiple program goals.

Exhibits and Displays

Exhibits and displays are the most frequently used form of programming in school library media centers. Surprisingly, however, many media specialists do not realize that this common format constitutes a program. When discussing our book with media specialists, one claimed that she had not developed a program in years. However, in a subsequent conversation, she described an activity she developed with student art. As mere decoration, artwork is not a program. But by adding a learning component, she made it one. To that end, simply displaying books on art technique and offering supplemental materials (brochures about nearby art museums, information about local artists' exhibits) near the students' work transform an aesthetically appealing exhibit into an effective and easy-to-prepare program.

Photo 2.1. Elaborate displays can combine many disciplines, including literature, media, and special events, as in this vibrant display case acknowledging the 100th anniversary of L. Frank Baum's *The Wizard of Oz*.
(Neshaminy Middle School, Langhorne, Pennsylvania, Neshaminy School District)

Exhibits and displays can be designed for most themes, whether supporting curriculum or personal interests. Common forms include:

- bulletin boards
- wall displays
- mobiles
- display cases
- display shelves
- table exhibits
- freestanding displays
- traveling trunks

Exhibits and displays are so versatile and easy to develop that some school library media specialists use them to feature different topics each month or grading period. Others create them to supplement large presentations. Before a major program, exhibits and displays introduce key concepts and can pique students' curiosity. During the event, they enhance the presentation. When used as follow-up activities after a program, they reinforce or extend learning. Finally, they are the perfect place to display books related to the program topic.

Because of their simplicity and familiarity, these formats make perfect first programs. Display cases, table displays, or bulletin boards attract patrons to the school library media center. Even though they seldom require much time to construct, they demand good planning if they are to be effective. Remember, placing items in a display case or hanging art on a bulletin board is not programming without a learning component.

Adding a learning component is not difficult. Simply plan your displays around a particular topic, develop learning objectives, and then create an activity, quiz, game, or assignment that allows students to demonstrate mastery. Make sure your displays are aesthetically appealing and are also rich in content. Label objects with titles and include descriptions to enrich student vocabulary. Provide curriculum-related information. Include challenging activities that inspire patrons to explore further reading opportunities.

Exhibits and displays are particularly useful for attracting students who would not otherwise want to visit the school library media center. Intriguing displays may draw reluctant students into the media center and invite them to explore what it can offer. Ideally, these students may even check out a book on the topic. Don't be surprised if they draw in faculty members as well.

A library media specialist from Michigan created an interactive bulletin board where students matched the motion picture depicted on a movie still with the title of a book upon which the film was based. More than one faculty member admitted that they were passing by the library media center when the still of a dashingly posed Denzel Washington drew them away from their destination and straight to the display for a closer look. While it became a running joke among faculty members, it proved to the media specialist that well-selected display items really can bring in new, sometimes unexpected patrons.

Chapter 2 contains information about identifying special exhibits and displays to meet specific thematic needs. For step-by-step instructions about constructing displays, read *3-D Displays for Libraries, Schools and Media Centers* by Earlene Green Evans and Muriel Miller Branch (see citation in References).

Interest Centers

Interest centers are more elaborate variations on displays or exhibits. Many classroom teachers, especially in science and occasionally in the visual arts disciplines, routinely construct classroom interest centers to supplement, reinforce, and enrich a unit. Consider using this form of programming in your school library media center. Like exhibits and displays, interest centers can attract students, supplement and extend learning, and provide follow-up activities after special programming events. Although they serve the same purpose as exhibits, interest centers are usually more elaborate. They often include several activities, supporting posters, instructions, artwork, and other resources.

You can build them in individual carrels, on tabletops, within divider units, or in any space large enough for independent or small group activities. You can erect them throughout the library media center. Interest centers should include intriguing items that stimulate thought and prompt discussion among students. For example, an aquarium in the media center that is set up and maintained by the science department can be the focal object for an interest center that provides activities on sea life or environmental issues.

To set up an interest center:

1. Select a versatile theme or topic. (You may want to leave the center up for a long time.)

2. Carefully define the goals.

3. Select your resources.

4. Use durable materials.

5. Make the setup functional and aesthetically appealing.

Find unique places to set up your interest center. For example, media specialist Barbara Lawrence made good use of the space beneath the stairs in her two-story library by creating a social studies interest center featuring a wall that resembled an old automat. She filled each compartment of clear, stackable chests of drawers with different artifacts, books, pictures, and information cards concerning various decades. For example, for the 1930s she included a newspaper article about breadlines, a photo of people living in "Hoovervilles," a British World War II cap, and copies of books including *Gone with the Wind,* biographies of FDR and Eleanor Roosevelt, and a volume about famous trials with the Lindbergh kidnapping case pictured on the cover. Trivia cards asked questions related to that era, and included notations for reference book resources, periodical database search topics, or Web site addresses that could lead to the answers.

Students were encouraged to complete the answer sheets provided, and then place them in a raffle bowl from which the media specialist would pick one winning entry per month. Prizes were related to the decade and included everything from a copy of the video from the original *Planet of the Apes* movie to a roll of bicentennial quarters. Many students were excited about the game and the prizes, but even students who cared about neither were intrigued by the display items. As Barbara had hoped, many of the books she'd placed in her "History Wall" drawers stayed in circulation much more than they would have on their usual shelves.

When identifying stimulating learning-center activities, consider topics that will interest students such as the following:

- aviation
- detectives
- computers
- careers
- music
- sports
- fantasy

- farming
- arts
- ecology
- interior design
- folklore
- crafts
- authors

Demonstrations

Programs may include you, or a guest speaker, demonstrating a process in person. As another possibility, you may also invite students to the school library media center to view a previously filmed demonstration. Your program can include one or multiple demonstrations. For one event in Louisiana, a program on silk screening focused on a local artist. After the demonstration, the media specialist hung samples of the artist's work throughout the media center, and art teachers followed up with classroom lessons where students created their own silk-screen designs.

The program was so successful that the media specialist expanded it the following year by inviting three different artists to demonstrate their unique art techniques: silk screening, painting with watercolors, and graphic designing on a computer. For this particular program the media specialist established three different centers (or stations). Small groups of students visited each center, learned about the art technique, viewed the art forms on display, and took part in hands-on activities planned by each artist.

Demonstrations can be developed around almost any theme, such as

- cooking
- using computer software
- silk screening
- cartoon drawing
- dancing
- puzzle solving

- baking
- scrapbook (or "memory book") designing
- Internet communication
- CPR
- exercise

Media Programs

Commercially produced media materials can support almost any thematic program. As important, they are usually easy to acquire and are often affordable to purchase or rent. Films, recordings, and computer software that focus on YA books and authors, special holidays, community resources, and other topics can become programs or program components. Likewise, media presentations make effective professional development programs for faculty members.

Featured Speakers and Entertainers

Programs covering all kinds of themes can benefit from guest speakers. Unquestionably, programs with exceptional guest speakers are among the most effective and memorable. You may invite one or several speakers to share information on a single topic. At a recent school library media center event, for example, an animal enthusiast shared information on reptiles and brought along his pet snakes and iguana as part of his demonstration. For a more elaborate approach, you might consider inviting a veterinarian, a zookeeper, a Society for the Prevention of Cruelty to Animals (SPCA) worker, and a pet obedience school instructor to share information on the proper care of domestic pets.

Programs featuring guest speakers offer several format options such as

- single speaker presenting the topic to one group
- single speaker presenting the topic multiple times to various groups
- multiple speakers presenting their topics to one group
- multiple speakers presenting their topics multiple times
- multiple speakers presenting their topics in different areas of the facility at the same time on the same topic.

CONCLUSION

Choosing from the many program formats available is simple once you have clearly defined your program needs, audience interests, and learning objectives. To further aid you in deciding the best formats, consider the target audience and time frame for the event. With these factors in mind, you can effectively begin the process of developing your program. New facets to your program and unexpected resources will inevitably improve your original plan, so modify as necessary. As the expert, you will know what changes will enhance your program and make it greater than you originally thought possible.

3

Final Stages of Program Planning

W ith your specific goals and much of your support coming together, you will now be able to complete the other stages of program development.

Once the leadership committee encouraged me to proceed with my program plan, I next needed to decide when we should have the event. After checking the school calendar, and talking with the book fair representative and fine arts teachers with students who would participate in the program, I set the date for the Tuesday of the first week in December. Although previously we always had our book fair in November, this December date allowed us to use a theme centering around the upcoming winter holidays.

During several goal setting sessions with my colleagues, we determined that, in order not to offend any students or parents of any religious group, we called the night "Winter Wonderland." This theme could easily be carried out with decorations of snowflakes, reindeer, etc.

Once the program idea had a date, theme, and support from staff and administration, the ideas just started to flow and the excitement began to grow.

OUTLINING
THE PROGRAM CONTENT

There were several points I wanted to keep in mind when planning the Winter Wonderland event. First, I wanted to provide parents a nighttime opportunity to browse through the book fair. I also wanted our fine arts programs to have the chance to perform for visiting parents. With these two goals in mind, I began contemplating a night of music combined with the book fair.

Photo 3.1. School library media specialist Holly Blaylock opens her music-themed book fair with a rendition of "Winter Wonderland."
(Killough Middle School, Houston, Texas, Alief Independent School District)

To begin the evening, I would sing "Winter Wonderland" and other holiday favorites. To keep the entire evening within a two-hour limit, I began to plan portions of the event that would facilitate the movement of several people among different settings where students would perform and the book fair books would be displayed. To keep the divisions clear, I decided to use different winter songs to mark the times of the evening. (For example, at 6:45, "Sleigh Bells Ring" led to the handbell choir's performance. At 7:30, "Deck the Halls" introduced a combined performance by the band, choir, and orchestra. At 8:00, "Dance of the Sugar Plum Fairies" brought in the dance team for their number, and we ended the evening with the "Jingle Bell" browse, where parents could look at the books from the fair before leaving for the night.

In the early planning stages, you will determine your theme, goals, audience, time frame, and available resources. With those elements in place, you can then choose the specific content and only the most relevant resources for your program.

With your content and goals in mind, begin your research. Talk to teachers, examine reference materials and professional resources, and explore the burgeoning data available over the Internet. During this stage, ideas will begin to solidify into a concrete program plan. A clear vision invites better communication and allows you to ask the right questions for securing resource persons, businesses, organizations, and potential helpers.

OBTAINING ADMINISTRATIVE APPROVAL

Throughout every planning stage, I met continually with my principal to discuss the evening and to secure her permission on many details, including the order of program events, refreshments, and crowd movement. When the program plans became more concrete, we further discussed how the evening's events would evolve, especially when she would introduce certain groups for performing and when she or both of us would make formal announcements to begin and end the event.

Before attempting to solidify specific program plans, know your district's policies about program development. Although you probably will not need permission to create curriculum-related programs formatted as centers, exhibits, or displays, you likely will need administrative approval for larger events that incorporate guest speakers or rented exhibits. Follow the correct chain of command so you can bring to life your ideas with the proper support from administration. In most cases, you would begin by securing your principal's permission concerning any activities, from inviting guest speakers to renting freestanding displays.

Once you've chosen the theme and you have a general vision of program content, share your ideas and goals with the principal. School districts are often concerned about specific themes and content of programs, particularly those not directly related to the school curriculum. Keep the principal or administrators apprised of all upcoming events. Always let them know about program plans, focusing especially on the positive PR they generate for the school.

After every visit, send a memo outlining your discussion and thanking the principal for his or her time and receptivity. As important, invite the principal to every program. For smaller events, such as exhibits or displays, informally ask the principal to visit your library media center. When hosting an elaborate program, send your principal a written invitation. Even if the principal slips in for a brief moment to observe a sliver of a presentation or view a display of students' work, including the principal establishes a positive rapport. Over time, even a handful of small programs can make a lasting impression.

Usually, principals are pleased when their media specialist takes the initiative to develop special programs for students and teachers. Even principals who do not become directly involved with you to create and develop programs will stop in for a quick visit during the event and see firsthand how exciting your media center is for students. Many who cannot collaborate may lend support in other ways, such as offering promotional ideas and even financial backing. Naturally, funding from the principal can enable you to achieve many program goals that would otherwise strain your budget, or be unattainable.

SECURING TEACHER SUPPORT

Fortunately, the focus and format of the Winter Wonderland program lent itself to easily attaining teacher support. The book fair and the numerous holiday concerts were already annual events at Killough Middle School. Consequently, by combining the events into one evening of entertainment and new books, I immediately obtained tremendous support from faculty. I included teachers, staff, and even students in various roles to ensure that everyone felt included and that everyone could contribute something meaningful to the event. Major participants included the following:

- The library aide helped with all planning, decorating, and promoting. Also, the aide primarily ran the book fair, oversaw the general program, and ensured that the evening's activities stayed on track.

- The fine arts team (band director, choir/handbell director, orchestra director) were responsible for student performances.

- The art department provided student art work.

- The dance instructor choreographed and led the dance team performance.

- The drama teacher provided props from the winter play and helped decorate the stage for the students' musical performance.

- The speech/debate teacher helped with sound and stage decoration.

- Other teachers donated refreshments and volunteered to help with serving or cleanup (they signed up for 30-minute intervals), crowd control, and the movement of more than 800 persons to the three areas of the school where portions of the program transpired.

Successful programs need faculty support. Throughout the development stages of program planning, request teacher input for the upcoming event. Their feedback can significantly improve your program, and contributing teachers develop a sense of ownership and excitement about the event. Such enthusiasm can create a ripple of excitement that spreads throughout your entire campus. Simple marketing strategies such as the following can generate great enthusiasm for the project:

- Share the upcoming program idea with the faculty members involved.

- Encourage faculty members to suggest program ideas and create related classroom activities.

- Provide faculty members with sample activities related to the program.

- At a faculty meeting, share with teachers the program theme and plans for the specific target group.

- Inform faculty members that you will continue making program announcements throughout the planning process.

- Finally, to avoid resistance from uninvolved parties, invite all colleagues to suggest program ideas that you might explore in a future program.

PLANNING THE SPECIFIC DETAILS

Because they depend on many factors, including the rigid schedule to which most schools must adhere, determining a date, time, and location for your event will sometimes require creative negotiation. The added challenge of scheduling human and material resources increases potential conflicts. Fortunately, as a media specialist you are accustomed to handling multiple responsibilities simultaneously and working around others' less flexible time constraints. As a result, this stage requires only some extra planning and diplomacy.

Select and Verify a Location

I met with the fine arts director several times to develop and then finalize program details. To accommodate both the book fair and the musical performances, we knew that the library media center alone would not do. After some discussion, we determined that the best plan would be to divide activities among three different areas: the school library media center, the commons area, and the cafeteria, which includes a performance stage.

In addition to securing these three areas, we printed out maps for program guests. We also asked the custodians to close off certain hallways to keep crowds in the designated areas.

After securing the principal's approval and support, choose the best location for your program. Conveniently, your school library media center will accommodate most events, simultaneously fulfilling learning objectives and publicizing the media center. By inviting students into the facility for a riveting program, you encourage them to perceive your media center as a vibrant hub of activity filled with interesting materials. Usually, such events are by far the most motivating tool for reaching students who rarely frequent the school library media center. A truly meaningful program that captures their attention and stimulates their curiosity will often inspire them to return later to browse through materials or view displays, even if they never check out a book.

Some program topics are best served in settings beyond the school library media center. For example, a traveling Shakespearean troupe might need the auditorium. Although it will be tempting to plan all events in the familiar surroundings of your own school library media center, sometimes another environment can prove more appropriate for the size of your audience, the theme of your program, or the activities to be shared. Consequently, when planning a program, consider on-campus options such as classrooms, labs, the school patio, or even the ball field. You may also schedule events off campus, as in the case of a North Carolina media specialist who organized a program for faculty members at the district professional library. Handle off-campus programs as you would a field trip: secure transportation, complete appropriate permission slips, and adhere to other district rules and policies.

Choose and Confirm a Date and Time

Scheduling an event is like constructing a three-dimensional puzzle. All facets must align and interlock or the entire structure collapses. So, at the earliest reasonable opportunity, secure a precise date for your program. Reaching that concrete decision, however, requires first selecting several tentative dates and times that might work, then coordinating them with other campus events on the school calendar. Determine two possible dates that do not conflict with other school programs, then investigate the following factors:

- school schedule (classes, lunch, passing periods)
- availability of resource persons
- availability of faculty members
- availability of support personnel, including volunteers and aides
- availability of resource materials that support the presentation

With these restrictions in mind, schedule small programs at least four to six weeks ahead of the program date. Schedule the extravaganzas several months in advance.

Working around the school calendar, particularly class schedules, can present another obstacle to planning. As an educator, your experience working around class, lunch, athletics, and fine arts schedules will help you choose the best date. Because having the teachers support your program contributes meaningfully to its success, be sure to discuss the matter thoroughly with colleagues at department chairperson, subject area, and faculty meetings.

Two major purposes for having a program are to create positive impressions of the library media center and to improve its effectiveness in the school. Understandably, most teachers are inconvenienced by disruptions to their schedule. By getting their input as you schedule the event, you engender a positive attitude toward you, the program, and your library media center. If you want your scheduling puzzle to come together and hold securely, allow teachers to contribute and feel good about being involved in a program. If they perceive it as just another imposition, your efforts to positively impact your target audience could backfire.

Select and Schedule Guest Speakers

If you've ever hosted a program involving guest speakers, you were probably pleasantly amazed to discover how many excellent speakers came from your local community. To learn the best ways to locate such speakers, see Chapter 4. For speakers from beyond your immediate geographic area, use the tips from Chapter 6, which go a step further and list Web sites of authors, publishers, and other resources that can connect you with speakers.

Selecting appropriate speakers is critical for programming. Above all, guest speakers must be interesting to students. Their content should be engaging and appropriate to the age level of the audience. With your professional experience, you can determine quite a bit about the potential speaker's ability to relate to a middle-school-aged audience. Professionals who exude energy and authority make vibrant, often entertaining presenters. Because programs that incorporate guest speakers depend entirely on their effectiveness, take the time and energy needed to pick the best speakers for your program audience.

We all know how deadly a bad speaker can be. Most of us have listened to excruciatingly dull speeches or abysmal presentations by speakers with poor communication skills. The topic may have been relevant, the material well organized and useful, but the speaker simply could not connect with the audience. For adults, that can be frustrating. With adolescents, it can be disastrous. Even speakers with solid professional credentials, an impressive body of knowledge, and plenty of speaking experience may not be the best choice for middle school students. Thus, prior to the program, determine whether the resource person is a good match for your patrons.

How can you make that decision confidently? Although no strategy is foolproof, certain practices in the business world apply here. Though requesting a resume or letters of recommendation from a community volunteer is unnecessary in this context, the principles behind them work. Choose people with experience speaking to young audiences. Guests who talk down to them, even unintentionally, can undermine all of your program preparation. To avoid these problems, get recommendations from colleagues who have already heard the speaker, or inquire about the speaker's prior engagements. It's not unreasonable to follow up on that request by calling the previous host. Courteously inquire about the general success of the program and about the guest speaker's strengths. By keeping the conversation positive, you make the previous host comfortable enough to share honest feedback. Whenever possible, meet with the potential speaker before making a definite commitment. During your conversation, you may wish to address these questions in whatever way you're comfortable:

- Is the speaker knowledgeable about the topic?
- Will the speaker be interesting to middle school students?
- Has the speaker worked with this age group before?
- Does the speaker seem to grasp the focus and purpose of my program?
- Have others recommended this speaker?
- Is the speaker genuinely willing to work within the program demands?

As a general rule, the most important question to consider is: If I were a student required to sit through this speaker's presentation, would I enjoy it as well as learn from it?

To find speakers, start searching near the school. The local community is filled with resource possibilities. County and city officials can make strong impressions on students. Artists, musicians, and athletes hold special intrigue for many students. Professionals at nearby businesses are often glad to share their time and expertise. Parents are also wellsprings of information.

The speaker's availability is a major consideration for program planning. When first meeting or conversing with potential speakers, discover when they will be available to participate in the program. If you have already chosen a date and location, share that information. If the date conflicts with the speaker's schedule, then suggest the alternate date still open on the school events calendar.

After selecting a speaker, share the following program details:

- date and time
- location of presentation
- program goals
- program content
- length of the program
- age of the audience
- size of the audience
- equipment and software needs (including microphone)
- accessory needs (such as podium, screen, dryboard and markers)

One week prior to the event, help your guest speakers by

- providing a final written reminder of date, time, and location
- reiterating the importance of being on time
- reminding them of the amount of time allotted
- confirming equipment and requested resources.

Finally, follow up with a telephone call several days before the event to ensure that they know and can honor their commitment. Clarify again their equipment needs and answer any final questions they may have.

As the central factor in this type of program, your guest speaker's commitment solidifies the tentative plans for date and time you made earlier. Immediately after guest speakers confirm their participation, lock in the program time on the school calendar. Because so many special events occur throughout a school year, other faculty members may be vying for some of those same times. Confirming your date will free up your alternative choice for other colleagues waiting to plan a special event (like a sports tournament, fair, or field trip).

Choose and Provide for
Support Personnel

In addition to all the teachers who filled specific roles in presenting the program, many parent volunteers helped with other important tasks. Some donated refreshments (almost 2,000 cookies), decorated tables, served, and cleaned. Others kept an eye on the merchandise while program guests visited the book fair.

Students helped out as well. Members of the student club, Young Sophisticates, helped decorate the school library media center for the event by putting up a Christmas tree, hanging garland, and stringing lights. The Young Leaders and National Junior Honor Society helped parents and students get to the right locations and then moved chairs when a larger crowd than we expected arrived for the musical performances.

In addition to participating in the concert, my eight student library helpers assisted with all phases of the program by setting up book fair items, decorating, designing promotional posters, cutting postcards for student announcements, moving furniture, and serving refreshments.

Even the custodial staff contributed by setting up furniture, cleaning, and blocking off areas where visitors weren't permitted (such as unsupervised classrooms).

Most important, the administrative staff also helped. The principal and three assistant principals helped with crowd control, served beverages, and led many performing students to their proper places at the right time. Best of all, the principal acted as Mistress of Ceremonies, which relieved me of a great deal of stress and was great PR for the media center and school.

Finally, because we were dealing with money and large crowds, we had peace officers present. Although we never encountered any problems, having them there was very reassuring.

Once you have the main guest speaker, you can find and secure other program contributors. You may need other guest participants, parent volunteers, and faculty members to help shoulder the responsibilities of executing your program. To determine how many presenters and helpers you need, consider how many students are attending and how many activities you have planned. While there is no set ratio that will always work, it is reasonable to have a few support members to help you coordinate the event, and, if possible, at least one on hand to assist each of the guest speakers.

Although it's not as demanding, finding volunteer help is similar to selecting primary guest speakers. Some larger schools may have enough staff members employed in the school library media center to shoulder all the supporting tasks, like ushering students in and out of the facility, operating equipment, and helping presenters with their displays and demonstrations. Regardless of their role, volunteers are essential members of your program team. Well before the program day, meet with all staff members and volunteers to give them information about the topic being presented. Assign each volunteer a specific task for which they are in charge and take time to review their responsibilities with them. Encourage them to ask questions. Staff members may know how you run the school library media center, where everything is and how it works, but your volunteers may be new to the campus, or to participating in programs. Help them feel secure and comfortable. As soon as they do, they can be more productive and effective.

Finally, ensure that each individual can relate to students. Though not as critical as the main guest speaker who will be commanding the students' attention, other participants help set the tone for the event. Volunteers who help students feel at ease and successful will greatly enhance the impression students come away with by program's end.

Select, Order, and Schedule
Resource Materials

The most common materials used to support programming include books, reference materials, professional materials for teachers, media, computer and audiovisual (AV) equipment, Internet Web sites, exhibits, and displays. (Chapter 4 focuses on identifying resources.) As mentioned previously, begin searching for support materials on the topic within your own school library media center, other media centers within the district, and the district professional library (if one is available). Then search the community for resource persons, businesses, and organizations that can provide support materials. When necessary, purchase books and materials related to the topic.

Being familiar with existing resources on your topic allows you to select, order, and schedule the materials. It is entirely appropriate to plan some programs around topics for which you already have great resources. This approach is especially helpful if your budget is extremely limited. When selecting resources, ask yourself:

- Is the content of the resource related to the program theme?

- Is the resource appropriate for the age level of the target group?

- Will the resource interest the target group?

- Is the resource current?

- Is the resource easily accessible?

- What is the cost of the resource (if any)?

Some media specialists begin planning an event a year in advance, particularly when anticipating an extravaganza such as a special anniversary of their school. Planning ahead enables you to budget for books and media in advance or reserve freestanding exhibits and multimedia programs. Naturally, if you're just beginning to incorporate programming into your routine, you may want to work with more short-term plans first. But as you become more adept at programming and as you begin repeating successful program themes, such advanced planning will come as naturally as keeping a list of book titles to order next year, or anticipating how you will adjust your budget next year to repair or replace equipment that you've noticed is in poor condition.

Develop Contingency Plans

Be ready to troubleshoot when unexpected challenges arise. Prepare alternate plans and backup activities. For smaller programs, also determine another date to present your program in case an unforeseen conflict arises. For larger events that lock in a date on the school events calendar, your alternate plan requires having backup activities ready. In either case, communicate clearly to all participants that they must notify you immediately if any schedule conflicts arise. Establishing clear expectations can prevent some troubles, but inevitable frustrations like unexpected illness or uncooperative weather demand contingency plans.

COMPLETING FINAL PREPARATIONS

By this stage, you've

- chosen a program topic
- determined learning objectives
- set goals
- planned activities
- selected the audience, location, and time of the event.

Now you are ready to plan the program day.

Identify, Select, and Prepare
Student and Parent Volunteers

Although elementary school media specialists often have many regularly scheduled parent volunteers, you will probably have to recruit assistants for major programs. Rather than seeking support only for the day of the event, line up volunteers to help before, during, and after the program. If you have parent volunteers, you probably found them by surveying parents at the beginning of the year. For special programs, return to the surveys you've kept on file and telephone parents who expressed interest in volunteering at special events. Also ask the Parent Teacher Association (PTA) or the Parent Teacher Organization (PTO) to support the program by finding volunteers for this one occasion. Regardless of how you recruit them, good volunteers significantly lessen your workload and your anxiety.

After securing helpers, have a meeting where you assign volunteers specific responsibilities. Always, your main goal is to find the best person for each program task. In the process, you must also help volunteers become clear and comfortable with their job in the program. Therefore, during the meeting

- establish a friendly yet businesslike rapport
- provide an overview of the upcoming program, including date and time
- build enthusiasm for the program throughout the meeting

- express clearly your vision for how the program day will evolve
- make certain all volunteers understand that they will work during the preparation stages as well as the day of the program
- explain what volunteer positions need to be filled
- tell volunteers that you value their input
- give volunteers an opportunity to choose what they want to do
- fill all volunteer positions
- discuss the tasks required of each volunteer.

Before the day of the event, volunteers can

- help with publicity (make posters, signs, and banners; write articles for newspaper)
- research the topic
- help locate resources
- assist in developing book displays
- decorate the facility
- hang artwork
- help create enrichment activities to follow the program
- help design interest centers.

On the day of, or during the program, volunteers can

- arrange furniture
- operate audiovisual equipment and computers
- serve as hosts and greet guests
- monitor traffic flow
- help with lighting
- remind classes of assigned times to arrive at program.

Publicize the Event

We publicized the Winter Wonderland program in many ways.

- Students assisted us in making posters that we hung throughout the campus.

- We had our broadcast team make announcements every morning for two weeks leading up to the event.

- We sponsored a poster/flyer contest in the school library media center to obtain some posters to disperse in businesses around the community.

- Two days prior to the program, we made short announcements for students to take home to their parents.

Our announcements read:

You're Invited

to

Killough Middle School's

Winter Wonderland

Tuesday, December 5

6:45 - 8:45 p.m.

Students, parents and staff are invited to attend an evening of holiday fun, books and the arts. The library is hosting a book fair where you can purchase great holiday gifts and show support for the KMS library. The Fine Arts Department will be showcasing the Handbell Choir, Chorale, Concert Band, Symphonic Band, and Orchestra. Student artwork and performances by the KMS Elegant Eagles dance team will also be highlights for the evening. Join us as we celebrate the season and share in the exciting programs of Killough Middle School.

For an event to be successful, you must advertise it. Early in the process, get backing from the principal and teachers. Their enthusiasm for your special event helps inspire students. (In most cases, students are the intended program audience, so direct all publicity toward them.)

Publicity targeted to students can include posters, daily announcements, newsletters, and advertisements on a marquee (if your school has one). Publicize the event in your school newspaper by asking a student to write an article about the program topic or inviting a student reporter to interview you. If publications exist at the district level, notify the administrative communications department about the upcoming event.

Find fun ways to get students involved in the advertising campaign. Consider sponsoring a poster contest. Invite a class, group, or club to design invitations to send to parents, administrators, and community members. Let another group create fliers to post around the school. Discover what advertising strategies are permissible on your campus and most effective to your target audience and plan accordingly. This stage is often the most fun and effective. Students love to contribute to these kinds of activities, and their participation creates some of the best PR for your program.

Not only do the final products promote the event, but the students' prior knowledge of it also creates a word-of-mouth campaign that can be especially effective. As we all know, it's one thing for students to see an adult's enthusiasm for an upcoming educational event. It's quite another for them to see that same enthusiasm from their peers. Students have a myriad of hobbies and interests about which they are thrilled to share information. From pets to sports to collections to unique ethnic or family traditions, students have vast expertise that could fit appropriately into a program that fellow students would relish.

When planning an extravaganza, inform local newspapers or even television stations. If you have never done so before, contact the communications department for your district, or find out from your Campus Communicator (on-site PR person) how to secure coverage of your event. If neither of these options works, ask one of your volunteers to take pictures during your event. Afterward, get the parents of students who appear in the pictures to sign release forms, then send the photos and a publicity sheet to the newspaper.

Remember that newspaper staffs work by strict deadlines and have many considerations for what is newsworthy. The timing of your event or even the number of articles they've recently published about your school or district may determine whether your submission is printed. Whatever their policies, respect them. If they work into your plans, capitalize on them. If they do not work this time, just learning about them can help when you plan subsequent events.

Whether through television, newspapers, or even simple letters to parents, let community members know what your media center is offering. It reflects well on you and your school.

Prepare Students and Teachers for the Event

Throughout the week of the program I checked on all groups to ensure that everyone was clear about the schedule. The music instructors and I rehearsed several times with all the performing students, focusing exclusively on the grand finale for two of the before-school rehearsals.

The day before the event, I posted announcements in the teachers' lounge and sent e-mail messages reminding teachers of the times they signed up to volunteer. In the e-mail I also reminded them where and when to bring their refreshment donations.

Target teachers in your publicity blitz as well. Prior to many programs, teachers need to give students background information on the topic. For example, before a guest author arrives for a program, consider giving your target audience's English teachers copies of that author's books. Plan with those teachers some activities that inform students about the author and the author's best and most recent works. Not only will students get more out of the program if they have this prior knowledge, but they will also ask more intelligent, relevant questions of the author.

Media specialist Greta Lawry included an impressive touch to her author programs worth imitating. She purchased a plaque listing the name of each guest author and the date of their visit. Over time, the plaque—a who's who of YA authors—became fine publicity when guests visited her media center. (Many YA authors' Web sites are listed in Chapter 6.)

Schedule Classes

If your program targets classes where nearly every student is in one grade level, scheduling is relatively simple. When planning programs for multiple grades, you must take into account all affected schedules, including music, athletics, and lunch. Whoever your target audience is, involve teachers in the scheduling process from the beginning. Understandably, teachers can be more flexible if they have been apprised of program plans from the start. Again, their support and cooperation are essential to scheduling your event.

Different types of programs often influence scheduling.

- If the program is a display or exhibit, teachers may sign up to bring classes to the media center. When appropriate, let teachers bring classes at their convenience.

- If the program is an interest center, schedule classes to participate in the center or allow teachers to send small groups or individual students to the media center with a pass.

- If the program is a demonstration or presentation by a guest speaker, classes or select groups must attend at your designated time.

Whatever schedule you set, remind teachers about it up to the very morning of the event. Consider

- mentioning the program schedule at several faculty meetings before the event

- sharing the schedule with teachers at club or organization meetings

- sending out reminders on attractive flyers

- posting reminders in the teachers' lounge

- enlisting volunteers to help remind teachers about the schedule

- announcing the program over the intercom the day before and the day of the event.

ARRANGING THE FACILITY

The library aide, student assistant, and I arranged the library media center for the book fair and the musical performance. On one side of the media center we set up tables for the book fair and on the other side of the media center we set up rows of chairs. A large Christmas tree divided both areas. We used snowmen decorations throughout the media center to carry out the Winter Wonderland theme. The handbell choir set up their tables at the entrance to the media center. Because it is an open library media center with very few walls, their music carried across the room.

In the commons area, we set up tables for the audience to sit and enjoy their refreshments. Here, too, we carried out the theme with more snowmen. We decorated the stage in the cafeteria with a tree, garland, and props from an upcoming play that looked like a beautiful living room.

An attractive facility sets the tone for your program. Increase program success by decorating, arranging furniture, providing for traffic flow, and using technology.

Decorate

Well before the event, put up attractive bulletin boards, then leave them up during the program to enhance the atmosphere. Display books and objects related to the event. Choose decorations (balloons, memorabilia, student art) that set your desired tone. Let students participate by making and displaying decorations. They can make posters, banners, mobiles, and other art to hang on walls or from the ceiling. Display their written work as well. Mount essays and writing assignments on colorful backgrounds and hang them in prominent places. Frequently, you can plan your decorating strategies with student and parent volunteers, and then let them decorate.

Arrange Furniture and Seating

If possible, arrange the furniture the day before your program. If that's not possible, draw a diagram of the room arrangement so custodial staff and volunteers can quickly set up the facility on the day of the event. If you don't already, you might want to keep a diagram on hand of how you normally arrange your furniture throughout the year. That way, after the event your volunteers can put everything back where it belongs. In addition, whenever others use your library media center for a special event and they rearrange your furniture, you can hand them the diagram and have them put your facility back in order so you don't have to do it yourself when they're done.

To arrange furniture and accommodate seating for your program, consider:

- Which volunteer is in charge of setting up the facility?

- Who will help arrange the furniture?

- Where should you place furniture being used for the program?

- Where should you place furniture not being used for the program?

- Where will the speaker stand?

- Will the speaker need a microphone?

- Will the speaker need a projection screen?

- Does the speaker have any special needs regarding seating arrangements or a speaker podium?

- How many students and guests will attend?

- Where will the students sit?

- Should classes sit together?

- Does your seating arrangement give all students an unobstructed view of the presenters?

- Where can you, teachers, and adult volunteers sit (or stand) so you can all monitor student behavior with minimal interruption to the speaker?

- Where will special guests (administrators, community members) sit?

- Do presenters require a place to sit?

- Who will help put the furniture back in order following the program?

Provide for Traffic Flow

You'll seldom encounter traffic flow problems when hosting programs for small groups. On the other hand, large events demand some creative planning to get students in and out of the facility expeditiously. To manage traffic flow, consider:

- When do I want students to arrive?

- Can all students arrive at once, or do I need to scatter arrival times?

- If I scatter arrival times, how will I notify teachers that it is time for them to bring classes? (I call? Volunteers call? Volunteers go to classes and escort students?)

- In what order should classes arrive?

- How much time will students need to be seated and to settle down?

- When should all students be seated and ready for the program?

- Do some students have special needs or considerations that must be addressed in advance? (For example, will students with physical challenges need to leave early?)

- Are a sufficient number of volunteers or student aides available to help supervise the traffic flow?

Use Technology Support

I arranged for sound systems in both the school library media center and the cafeteria. As media specialist, I'm in charge of the school sound system, so we were able to set up those systems early in the day and do sound checks to ensure that everything was in order by program time.

Today more than ever, some programs may depend entirely on technology. For example, showing an educational video can be a form of programming if it aligns with concrete learning objectives and includes follow-up activities and support materials. In most cases, however, technology supports other program formats. When you teach a concept using PowerPoint or a guest speaker uses an overhead projector or microphone to share information, technology acts as support.

Long before the day of your program, determine what equipment your guest presenters need. As a safeguard, give presenters a copy of your district copyright adherence policy. When you know exactly what equipment everyone needs, gather (or order) all equipment and software ahead of time. In some cases, technology materials must be scheduled weeks in advance.

When using multimedia, ask yourself these questions:

- What equipment do presenters need?
- Will presenters bring their own equipment?
- Is my requested equipment in good working order?
- What software do presenters require?
- Do they want a podium or table and chair?
- Do the participants need a dryboard, easel, or chart?
- Where should I place the equipment?
- Will the equipment need to be moved during the program?
- Do participants know how to work the equipment?
- Do they need someone to operate it for them?
- Who will take care of lighting?
- Do I have backup equipment, extension cords, and extra bulbs available and handy?

If you can, set up AV equipment, including computers, microphones, and software support, the day before the event. Test it to make certain it works properly. Check focus and sound levels from all areas in the facility where equipment will be used. Ensure that the screen, if one is needed, is positioned for optimal viewing wherever participants may be seated. Just before students arrive, test everything once more.

If presenters want to operate the equipment themselves, let them test the equipment so they feel comfortable using it. If they request a volunteer's assistance, be sure the volunteer is ready and knows what support the presenter needs. Address these concerns and do all last-minute troubleshooting before students arrive.

EXECUTING THE PROGRAM

The book fair was held in the school library media center with the handbell choir and poetry. It was here that I began the evening by singing "Winter Wonderland" and welcoming everyone to the event. Parents then had time to browse the book fair items. From there, the audience moved to the commons area, located near the library media center and cafeteria. Because there is no carpeting in that area, this is where volunteers served refreshments of cookies, punch, and Hershey's Kisses®. Later, guests moved onto the third part of the program, the student musical and dance performances in the cafeteria.

To ensure that we had time to include all student participants, we limited each group's performance to two songs. To end the concert, I began by singing a solo, and was joined in by all the groups until we ended with a grand finale of traditional holiday music.

Throughout the evening, we announced that everyone is welcome to browse through the book fair any time. We also played music in the library media center as guests browsed and purchased books. For this part of the program, the library aide and some trusted adult volunteers (including my husband) ran the cash register and helped guests select and purchase book fair items. Something essential that I also did was to arrange with one of the assistant principals to put the book fair money in the school safe at the end of the evening. Once the program was over, I was very ready to pack up and leave. Thanks to advanced planning, the assistant principal and I placed the money in the school safe and I could leave promptly after everyone else was gone.

For events requiring one or more speakers, tend to the following details on the day of the program:

- Remind teachers and students of program times and their seating times.

- Remind volunteers about the times and scheduling.

- Review with the volunteers their assigned tasks.

- Complete final seating arrangements.

- Check the environment: temperature, lighting, and ventilation.

- Make certain the speakers' requests have been met before they arrive.

- Greet the speakers.

- Make sure they are comfortable with equipment, room arrangement, program agenda, and schedule.

- Review with the speakers the importance of staying on the time schedule (if it's helpful, provide a signal to end the presentation).

- Spend some time after the program with the guests (coffee, lunch, short visit).

Present the Program

Even though several people share the responsibilities for your program, you are ultimately responsible for its success. To ensure that your event is executed precisely and professionally, follow these steps:

1. Begin at the scheduled time.

2. Welcome patrons and provide a brief introduction to the program topic.

3. Acknowledge everyone who contributed to the program.

4. Remind students of expectations for behavior and participation (for example, when it is appropriate during the program for them to ask questions).

5. Introduce the guest speaker.

6. Monitor students during the presentation.

7. Devise a subtle way of signaling to the speakers when their time is nearly over.

8. When each speaker has finished, thank him or her for the presentation.

9. At the end, thank everyone for attending.

10. With the help of your volunteers, instruct students and teachers on how and when they should leave the facility.

Follow Through After the Event

When the event is over, your program is not complete without appropriate reinforcement. To ensure that students get the most out of the program, provide follow-up activities. These activities should somehow review or extend the information presented in the program. The following options for media specialists and teachers will provide student enrichment.

*   Consider a follow-up event or demonstration on the same topic.

*   Make books on related topics available for checkout.

*   Make media on related topics available to teachers.

*   Provide enrichment activities (information centers, displays) in the school library media center.

*   Compile a Webography on your program topic and display it near the computers.

*   Encourage and suggest individual or classroom activities.

*   Give both students and teachers bibliographies of related student resources.

*   Give teachers a bibliography of related professional materials.

*   Request feedback from the students and teachers about the program (see Chapter 7 for details).

PROGRAM CHECKLIST

Several Months Prior to Event
_____ Decide theme/topic
_____ Develop objectives
_____ Identify available resources

One Month Prior to Event
_____ Obtain permission from administration
_____ Select participants
_____ Select materials
_____ Identify audience, date, and time
_____ Contact participants
_____ Begin publicizing event
Develop contingency plans:
_____ Alternate dates
_____ Alternate activities
_____ Alternate speakers

One or Two Weeks Prior to Event
_____ Schedule volunteers
_____ Determine seating arrangements
_____ Determine traffic flow
_____ Give teachers schedule of event
_____ Discuss event at faculty meeting (problems, schedules, etc.)

Day Prior to Event
_____ Prepare seating arrangement
_____ Prepare audiovisual equipment
_____ Arrange decorations, displays, and exhibits
_____ Remind volunteers and participants of time
_____ Remind teachers of schedule

Day of Event
Last-minute check of facility:
_____ Room temperature
_____ Lighting
_____ Room arrangement
_____ Audiovisual equipment and cords
_____ Speaker podium
_____ Seating arrangement
_____ Review individual duties with volunteers
_____ Greet speakers

After the Event
_____ Do informal evaluation
_____ Do formal evaluation
_____ Send letters of appreciation to participants
_____ Analyze program

Figure 3.1. Checklist for successful programs.

FOLLOWING YOUR PROGRAM CHECKLIST

Because there is so much to consider and do in programming, you will want to follow a structured checklist. It can help you organize your work and complete all necessary tasks for planning, presenting, and assessing your program. (See Figure 3.1.)

CONCLUSION

Because programs can be so varied, feel free to adapt your program plans to your current level of interest and experience. If developing a program is new to you and the process seems somewhat daunting, then start small. Even with a limited theme, audience, and format, your program can impact your participants significantly and inspire you profoundly. Consider inviting one speaker to present to a single class. Even simpler, create an interest center around an intriguing theme. For a nominal fee, you can even rent a pre-designed display from a museum or cultural organization (see Chapter 4 for more details) and include an additional learning element or two.

The possibilities are limitless. Create an interactive bulletin board or display. From those small beginnings, let your programs grow. The inspiration you'll feel from your initial successes will soon lead you to coordinate multifaceted programs that make lasting impressions throughout your school and community.

4

How to Identify and Locate Resources

In our global society, resource people and materials abound. Thus, with only a little knowledge and ingenuity, we can easily locate exceptional resources to support programming.

IDENTIFYING RESOURCES

At first, your resource options may seem either too vague or overwhelmingly broad. But as you search, you will quickly discover what types of resources exist, who has them, and when they are available. Do not become impetuous about acquiring resources too quickly. Sometimes one worthwhile discovery will lead to an even better program idea, or a less expensive or more creative and, thus, less difficult means of obtaining the resource when you actually need it. Limit the first part of your search to simply discovering what you can find, and the many places that have exactly what you want. To do so, you must first become familiar with all the resource possibilities available. The following list should set you firmly on your way.

Educational Resources

Even before you begin searching, become familiar with the various types of educational resources that support programming. Knowing about the major resource options that follow can give you a clear vision for the kind of program support to pursue.

Books

Books are the cornerstones of nearly all school library media programs. Often, a book or books will be the program topic. When it's not the primary focus, it should still be a major component. For example, if your event focuses on developing a skill, such as learning some new technology, you should still include books to help present the material or as supplements for further study. Keep books handy for introducing information before and during the program, and make them available for perusal or checkout after the program to extend learning. Because our primary goal as educators is to encourage lifelong readers, make books a central element of any program.

After gathering all book resources from your media center, extend your search to other media centers in your district. If you belong to a professional online networking organization (California, Florida, and Texas have prominent ones), you can collect resources statewide. Once you begin developing long-term visions for future programs, you may budget for and order resources to have on hand when you are ready to plan the event. Over time, your school library resource center can become noted for a particularly strong collection covering whatever topics you present most often. Conversely, as you search you will also learn which school library media centers specialize in resources on topics you might offer in the future. Keeping a note of such details will make future searches faster and more efficient.

Professional Materials

When gathering resources for programs, search your campus or district professional collection. Many of these books and journals explore education theory and share creative classroom activities. From them, you may find worthwhile information to supplement programs for students, or professional growth activities to use for programs directed to faculty. In doing our research for this book series, we discovered that many districts do not publicize their professional collections very well. You may be surprised to find a gold mine of resources immediately available to you in your own district.

Also, remember that teachers may have resources in their departments that you would not normally keep in your media center. Physical education equipment, history games, lab equipment, and class sets of novels could supplement a program in their respective subject areas.

Audiovisual Materials

Like any lesson, a program should meet the needs of visual, auditory, and kinesthetic learners. Eye-catching visuals, appealing graphics, and appropriate audio elements hold students' attention and enhance learning. After deciding what audiovisuals to incorporate in your program, begin gathering resources from your own collection. Videos, books on tape, and CD-ROMS that you initially ordered for classroom use may meet your program needs. As suggested earlier, expand your search incrementally.

Ask team leaders or grade-level coordinators if they have resources you need. If you have a regional distribution center that lends AV resources, check their catalog or Web site and order what you want well before the program. Order the material so it arrives before your program date. Preview the work to determine its quality and decide what parts you will include in the program. Better to get it early and request an extension than to discover that your well-timed order was never filled.

Also, consider AV material you wish to create. Attractive overheads complement your programs. Because they combine information, visual movement, and sound effects, PowerPoint presentations are outstanding teaching tools. Sometimes filming your own video personalizes the learning for students, especially if some have contributed to the effort. For example, when a media specialist in Oklahoma could not find a video that succinctly explained tools of early Native Americans, she and some students videotaped a demonstration with props and artifacts she had collected.

As you determine your AV needs, set aside or reserve equipment. You probably have much of what you need already. Gather it together and check it out to yourself. You don't want an assistant or volunteer to unknowingly issue the equipment to someone else just as you are prepared to use it. If a teacher already has equipment you want for your program, arrange early to get it back, or negotiate a plan to have a volunteer retrieve and return it.

More expensive equipment, such as a liquid crystal display (LCD) projector, may be more difficult to acquire. Some districts purchase one such item and then make it available to all campuses, or they limit its use to the administrative offices. Get an up-to-date list of your district's AV resources, and the policy for ordering them or checking them out. Sometimes, waiting lists make it impossible to secure the equipment you want unless you've requested it several months in advance.

Check with other school library media specialists. Some colleagues work closely together, each agreeing to order different AV resources and sharing them among campuses. Others have a central budget controlled by an administrative coordinator. At the very least, suggest that all media specialists in your district list the AV equipment they have and are willing to share, then distribute those lists at the next district meeting. Having immediate access to this list can save much time as you gather program resources.

Teacher- and Student-made Resources

As an educator, you probably create some support material from scratch. Making your own program resources, alone or with teachers and students, can benefit everyone. It is usually economical. It can give teachers a new focus on a familiar lesson. It can present students with a creative activity and give them a chance to contribute to your event. For example, instead of requiring individual students to write reports, a social studies teacher introduced his students to jackdaws (see description below) and allowed groups of students to compile them for his explorers unit. They gave their best projects to the media specialist, who displayed them in the library media center.

Jackdaws

A jackdaw is a type of portfolio used as a learning tool. Most often, jackdaws support the social studies curriculum. Whether teacher-made or commercially produced, they can contain reproductions of historical documents, artifacts, maps, photos, and other interesting educational materials that bring an historical figure or a period of history to life. Sometimes, in the language arts classroom, jackdaws can be used to enrich a literary link.

Jackdaws are frequently paired with information books, historical fiction, or biographies. For example, before or after reading a biography about Abraham Lincoln, students enjoyed examining the jackdaw related to Abraham Lincoln that included the following items: a photograph of Lincoln, a Civil War battlefield map, a log cabin, a miniature Union flag, and a copy of the Emancipation Proclamation.

During the program, jackdaws are attractive, interesting, and useful; afterward, they're easy to store. Although some media specialists keep jackdaws only for their programs and displays, many catalog them and allow teachers to check them out for classroom use. When planning a program for teachers, note that "Creating Jackdaws" is an excellent topic. Jackdaws are versatile, easy to compile, and yet, still unfamiliar to many teachers.

Display Boards

Rather than working with a flannel board, many middle school library media specialists employ the same concept using a tri-fold display board. Available at most teacher supply stores or through library or science catalogs, the tri-fold board can become the ideal forum for visually depicting stories during read-alouds. One media specialist read Sarah Stewart's *The Gardener* to classes of sixth-grade reading students. As she read, she added objects described in the text to the board until, by the end of the book, she had created an entire visual representation of what she'd just read.

Display boards can be used to create two-dimensional art or to serve as the backdrop for three-dimensional, multiple-part exhibits. Because they're portable and not too cumbersome, you can carry them with you to share programs in classrooms. They also store flat so they're easy to set aside for reuse later.

Student Art

Student art can impressively supplement programming while adding a personal touch that means a great deal to the contributing students. As decoration, student art can significantly enhance your media center. Student art correlates with programming on many levels. It can be the entire program focus, as in the case of bulletin boards or exhibits, or it can supplement a more expansive event. In collaboration with teachers, one library media specialist developed a different theme for each of seven months then asked teachers to assign art projects relating to the theme. On their designated month, students brought completed art to the school library media center and built displays of their work with the help of an adult volunteer. Some theme suggestions include:

ART PROGRAM THEMES

October	Haunted Library
November	What if the Turkey Actually Was Our National Bird?
December	The Greatest Gifts
January	Ice Castles
February	Presidents in Profile
March	Dreaming of Spring Break
April	April Fools

Keep in mind that students often enjoy creating art in unique formats, including manipulatives, jackdaws, and even three-dimensional examples of the monthly art project listed above.

Student Projects

While adding character to the school library media center and allowing students to display their work, student projects also enhance programming. With students' permission, the projects may be stored and used for future programs. Conversely, some library media specialists find students to create projects for upcoming programs.

Both strategies can work. Sometimes projects inspire program ideas. At other times, program planning involves allowing students to contribute projects that support the program goals.

Dioramas

Easy to make, usually compact, and aesthetically appealing, dioramas can really make a school library media center come to life. Instead of assigning book reports, many teachers allow students a more creative outlet, like making dioramas that can be displayed in the school library media center. After reading individual books, students can take an empty shoe box and depict a memorable scene using three-dimensional objects, self-generated drawings, and pictures cut out from magazines or printed from the Internet. Once their scene is complete, they cover the box opening with clear cellophane, and label their project with their name, book title, and author.

You can display dioramas on tables and shelves throughout the school library media center, but of course, you also want to make any books depicted in the dioramas available for check out. After all, in addition to being attractive, a diorama can also serve as a great motivator to get students to pick up books they might not otherwise read.

Interactive Bulletin Boards

Interactive bulletin boards are usually three-dimensional displays that attract patrons and encourage independent learning. They often have three standard components: (1) an intriguing title, (2) information that ties in with current learning, and (3) an interactive game or puzzle that requires students to use their new knowledge.

Photo 4.1. This interactive bulletin board invites students to win a chocolate kiss by guessing the country from which each heart-matted foreign word originated.
(Neshaminy Middle School, Langhorne, Pennsylvania, Neshaminy School District)

Such bulletin boards can be used in all disciplines. For a language arts program, one media specialist titled her board, "On a First Name Basis" and listed characters from both classic novels, such as Phyllis Reynolds Naylor's *Shiloh*, Allan W. Eckert's *Return to Hawk's Hill*, and several Gary Paulsen and Paul Zindel titles, as well as more contemporary works including Bill Wallace's *Coyote Autumn*, John H. Ritter's *Over the Wall*, and Alice McLerran's *Dragonfly*. Then she photocopied and cut out the titles from the actual book covers, mounted and laminated them, and set them beside the book tray beneath her bulletin board.

The interactive game required students to place each book title beside the character who appeared in the novel. To help students, the library media specialist listed every character alphabetically on a sheet of paper and provided character descriptions and a key scene from the story that demonstrated the traits described. While providing useful clues to a fun game, the details also shared enough information to pique students' curiosity and inspire them to check out one of the books, which were lined up in the book tray beneath the display.

Combining geography and science, another media specialist hung different rock samples from strings attached to a world map. Under each continent she placed a small clear plastic cup. Using sidebar information that described rock formations around the world, students were invited to place each rock sample into the correct cup. To check their accuracy, they lifted the one country outlined in red on each continent. Under it was a picture and the name of the correct rock.

Manipulatives

Manipulatives are to middle-school media centers what puppets are to elementary libraries. While many popular programs for elementary students involve using puppets, middle-school students generally find them too juvenile. However, manipulatives can be a perfect hands-on medium for interactive learning, especially for kinesthetic learners.

Manipulatives are any three-dimensional objects that can be (as the name implies) manipulated manually for multisensory learning. For example, an architectural scale model of a building that is merely constructed and painted is not a manipulative. But one that has working doors and windows and is constructed from samples of the actual materials of the building (glass, adobe, stone, concrete) that students can feel firsthand, is a manipulative. While some teachers consider plastic three-dimensional geometric figures manipulatives for classroom use, true manipulatives would allow students to construct and re-create shapes, such as circles that can be stretched into ovals, or squares that can be shifted into rectangles.

Such geometric figures and architectural scale models are examples of commercially designed manipulatives that can be purchased or rented. But more common and cost-effective are student- and teacher-made manipulatives. Eighth-grade classes required to read *Anne Frank: The Diary of a Young Girl* might build a scale model of the Amsterdam attic in which Anne and her family hid, including the skylight and the retractable bookcase built to camouflage the entrance to their living space. For seventh graders, consider constructing a scale model of the plane that crashes in the opening sequence of *Hatchet*. As stated above, a simple model airplane would not be a manipulative. However, if it has movable propellers, spinning wheels, and doors that open and close, it would be a manipulative.

While such manipulatives are commonly used for demonstration purposes during a program, they are especially inviting to students when left on display after the program is completed. Place them close enough to the circulation desk so you can monitor their use, but far enough away so students who genuinely want to experiment with them and learn independently can feel free to do so.

LOCATING RESOURCES

Now that you know many of the resources that support programming, your search will indicate who has them and when they are available. Set parameters for your search by answering three questions:

1. What do I want?

2. What can I afford?

3. When do I need it?

Your answers narrow your search and give it direction.

Your Campus

Every day at work, you're surrounded by outstanding program support. Often, materials in your own inventory are precisely what you need. Beyond the boundaries of your own library media center, your campus is filled with people and materials that make for great programming.

Your School Library Media Center

Begin gathering resources from your library media center. Frequently, books and materials in your collection will inspire program ideas or clarify your program focus. Knowing your collection well enables you to find books and materials easily. Seeing what you have on hand determines how deep and extensive your subsequent search must be.

Classrooms and Offices

After using all resource possibilities from your media center, expand your search incrementally. With a little investigating, you'll discover that many colleagues on your campus have expertise or collections appropriate for your program. A teacher or administrator may be your best choice for guest speaker. What a convenient treasure an expert on your own campus can be. There's no need to find, interview, and invite an unfamiliar speaker from the community if you have colleagues who relate well to students, are on campus already, and could enthusiastically share their knowledge about a favorite topic.

Colleagues may also share relevant support material from their departments or personal collections. For example, one library media specialist in Houston found enough materials on Texas history in the social studies department closet to decorate her entire facility for an event.

Similarly, another media specialist did the same with science equipment. When she realized how many science books arrived with her annual book order, she created a special display to highlight them. From the science department, she gathered beakers, goggles, and a rack of test tubes for one side of the display. On the other side, she spread dirt in a tray and sprinkled in pebbles, fake butterflies, a patch of grass, and leaves. To complete her scene, she went to the local dollar store and purchased candy worms, and plastic bugs and flowers. Making copies of an old treasure hunt that one of the science teachers no longer used (students had to find specific plants and insects common in their region) added the learning element that transformed one simple observation—an unexpected abundance of books on one topic—into a successful and inexpensive program.

Finally, class sets of novels from the language arts department or a grade-level coordinator's classroom can support programs. Depending on the nature and target audience of the program, sometimes having students read aloud excerpts from an author's work varies your program and encourages active participation.

Your District

Exploring other areas of your district beyond campus gives you access to still more resources that you can secure at no cost. Even as site-based management allots separate budget money to each school, the district administrative offices still have more financial resources than even the largest campuses. Even if they cannot supplement your program financially, they may have expensive equipment that you cannot obtain otherwise. Just as faculty and staff members in your building can be great resource possibilities, so too can administrators, teachers, and other media specialists throughout your district.

Administrative Offices

Your district administrative offices have human and material resources that can significantly impact your program quality. Your own limited budget might prevent you from ordering unique or elaborate equipment that is available through the district communications department. Although some individual library media centers have their own broadcasting equipment or facility, most do not. However, your administration might. Find out who coordinates district-wide inservice events, or find your district PR representative. Either of those staff members will probably have digital cameras, recording and projection equipment, and computer hardware and software for larger, more sophisticated program presentations.

Finally, realize that licensing for many computer software programs or Internet research databases is more cost-effective if purchased for an entire district or cluster of schools, rather than on a campus-by-campus basis. As a result, your district administrative offices may be subscribing to some services that you can add to your campus at no charge to you.

Although the administrative communications or technology department may inform each campus about the new acquisition, they seldom have the time to follow through on the installation without some consistent prompting by you. Therefore, inquire about which resources your district already pays for, and make sure you get access on your own campus. Even if you find out that the district is paying for access for some resources that wouldn't apply to your school, you at least have strong support for getting the district to pay for similar resources on your campus when you're ready to acquire them.

Professional Libraries

If you're fortunate to have one, check the district's professional library. It houses more extensive resources than you would keep in your inventory. Such libraries, which are often part of the district administration building or a separate Teacher Center, often have excellent resources to support programming. Many district libraries issue support materials, such as films and computer software. A few also offer research services that locate professional articles on your topic, identify information about authors, guide Internet searches, or secure appointments from available speakers. Even if they cannot make the arrangements for you, they may have a community resources file that includes possible speakers.

Other School Library Media Centers

You are probably already in close contact with other middle school media specialists in your district. Initiate a routine of informing each other about new resources by listing good program ideas and support material that you're willing to share. Ask your colleagues to do the same. If you don't already alternate campuses for your regular meetings, start. While visiting another media center, ask for a tour, especially of the storage, periodical, and AV rooms. You may be inspired by something that they never even thought to mention.

Realize that colleagues at elementary and high school media centers may also have materials worth acquiring. Elementary facilities are usually brimming with kits, games, decorations, and manipulatives that may work into a program. Although you are not likely to have your patrons play a game meant for elementary students, you might use game pieces or parts of kits to create your own activities.

Because high schools are often bigger and serve a larger student population, their budgets are also greater. As a result, sometimes a high school library media center may have reference materials, computer software, or AV equipment that you can borrow for a special program.

Other media specialists at any level may maintain diverse, full, and current community resources files. When accessing such a treasure, discuss programming ideas and resources with the other media specialist. If you already have a community resources file of your own, add to it with materials from your colleagues. If you don't have one, you can create one as you begin exploring the resources available throughout your community.

Community Resources

Regardless of its size, every community has many human and material resources to offer schools. Finding them depends upon what people, places, and special events exist in your community. Remember, community resources can either be the cornerstone of your program or provide supplemental support. In either case, they're worth finding and using.

Naturally, your program choices often reflect the beliefs, attitudes, and dreams of your students and their community. Until recently, smaller communities might draw from rich local archives while big cities had more high tech and diverse resource possibilities. With global communication and the Internet, however, populations at both extremes are now converging. If your school is older, you may need to borrow more sophisticated software that your budget cannot accommodate. Conversely, you probably have historical resources (books that are long out of print, and vertical file materials kept for historial appeal) that media specialists at newer schools would love to use as program support.

Finding resources requires knowing your community's people, historical sites, institutions, businesses, organizations and clubs, government agencies, and special holidays and events. Some programs evolve entirely around a single community resource, such as a guest speaker and a unique display. To support a schoolwide campaign against violence, a media specialist in Wyoming hosted a program about school safety presented entirely by the local peace officers. Other programs may require only supplemental support from the community. Following a meningitis scare in one southern U.S. community, a media specialist presented a program called "About Airborne Diseases" after which she distributed pamphlets collected from local doctors' offices and hospitals.

For this part of your search especially, be systematic. Chart a course for identifying and locating resources. Decide what you want, then list logical providers. Knowing budget, time, and space parameters will also help you decide what resources to pursue. Figure 4.1 lists resources available in most communities. Beyond these suggestions, consider resources unique to your community because of local traditions and industry.

Resource People

In every school and community, many resource persons are eager to share their knowledge, skills, and special interests with young people. Thus, you seldom need to search hard for community members eager to share their expertise. When searching, begin with the easiest to find: parents, teachers, and students in your own school. Many parents and faculty members are eager to share special talents, leisure activities, travel experiences, and career information. Whether you're looking for a guest speaker or a unique collection to feature in a display case, these resource people can provide excellent enrichment, usually at no cost.

If your campus has a social committee, they have probably surveyed teachers about hobbies, collections, and travel experiences. If not, suggest that someone start a committee. Or, send out a get-acquainted survey at the beginning of the year asking teachers to list hobbies that they might like to share with students. Common hobbies such as gardening or painting can enhance some programs as much as pastimes like birding or collecting antique toys.

Because other media specialists in your district may be investigating similar information at their schools, plan a sharing time during a meeting to let each other know about unique human resources at every campus. Sometimes people you've known only casually for years may have a unique talent worth using as program support. For example, at my district, the library media specialists met monthly. Although we were all friendly with one another, we tended to network only with colleagues from the same level of school. To my surprise, it wasn't until her retirement party that I learned that one of the high school library media specialists wrote and performed clever, hilarious songs. As she played the guitar and shared some songs, my mind reeled with great program possibilities. Before leaving the retirement party, I asked her if she would be willing to do school visits, then created an entire program around her endearing talent.

Ways to Locate Resources

Type of Resource	Sources
Resource People	Questionnaire PTA or PTO Faculty recommendations Public library
Interesting Places	Chamber of Commerce City guides Internet (see Chapter 6)
Institutions	Telephone directory Internet (see Chapter 6) Teacher/parent recommendations
Business and Industry	Telephone directory Chamber of Commerce Internet (see Chapter 6) Teacher/parent recommendations
Clubs and Organizations	Chamber of Commerce Directories Internet (see Chapter 6) Teacher/parent recommendation
Government Agencies	Internet (see Chapter 6) Telephone directory
Holidays and Special Events	Chamber of Commerce News media
Professional Materials	Selection aids
Displays and Exhibits	Museums, Businesses, Institutions, Organizations Media resources (magazines, television) Internet (see Chapter 6) Other libraries

Figure 4.1. Ways to locate resources.

Occasionally, community members may come to you to share their unique talents. More often, though, you will hear about them through others or read about them in local news features. Staying alert to extraordinary and even mildly interesting news items that you come across daily can lead you to program participants.

Consider professionals in the community (including parents) as possible program speakers. Writers, artists, doctors, architects, attorneys, pilots, scientists, and engineers are frequently invited to career days and may be receptive to speaking at other special programs. Government office holders and employees of institutions, businesses, and government agencies are usually top-level contacts; however, others in the community are also worth considering. Communities are overflowing with bright, active volunteers and retired persons who can provide enrichment on various topics. Members of local clubs and organizations or retirees who participate in specialized groups related to their former professions are wellsprings of information.

Interesting Places

Your community may seem so familiar that you have stopped noticing special places or even historic sights that might provide perfect program ideas or provide ideal resources. These sites may include tourist attractions, government buildings, landmarks, parks, gardens, fountains, and even shopping malls. Students frequently take field trips to places that could also enrich media programs by providing brochures, pamphlets, and speakers. Also, realize that local Chambers of Commerce usually have wonderful packets of material about cities and what they have to offer.

Institutions

Throughout your community are institutions with materials or resource people related to the middle-school curriculum and student interests. By targeting the right institution for your program, you can secure most of the materials or presenters you need with one telephone call. (Figure 4.2 highlights examples of institutions that frequently support programs in middle schools along with program titles that have worked well for media specialists.) (See Chapter 6 for Web sites of various museums and virtual tours of art galleries, zoos, and other interesting places.)

One especially worthwhile institution is the public library. What you don't have in your own media center, or cannot obtain through district interlibrary loan, may be available for checkout. As part of their outreach programs, city and county libraries frequently use programming to teach concepts or to increase public awareness of their facility. Consider joining a "Friends of the Public Library" organization (they have different names in different parts of the country) to continually be apprised of their programs and new PR strategies for attracting patrons.

Institutions	Program Titles
Bank	Small Deposits, Big Returns (How to Open and Use a Savings Account)
Fire Department	Fireproof Your Home
Hospital	Play it Safe: Preventing Sports and Recreation Accidents
Library	After School Programs for At-Risk Youth (county librarian presented to parents)
Museum	Computer Graphics: Art of the Future
Police Force	Scared Straight (youth crime prevention)
University	Reviewing Young Adult Books (professor presents program to faculty)
Zoo	Saving Endangered Animals

Figure 4.2 Examples of institutions with program titles.

Colleges and universities are also prime program resources worth special consideration. Although the gap between middle school and college may seem vast, it really isn't. As we all reach to inspire a generation of avid readers and lifelong learners, we can more easily see the benefits of closing that gap and helping students recognize the continuum of learning that, we hope, will last a lifetime. With that realization, know that colleges and universities can provide especially good resources for your programs. Additionally, they also host programs that either relate to youth, or can be adapted to meet the needs of a target audience at your school.

To find out what guest authors, art exhibits, or programs higher learning institutions offer to young audiences, look for university happenings in the newspaper or get on the university's mailing list. You might also contact the public relations department of local universities, or the cultural arts departments directly. If you simply pass such information on to teachers as possible field trip opportunities, you'll miss potential resources and ideas you can use yourself. In addition to just securing resources or generating program ideas, offer correlating events on your campus to pique student interest and expand their knowledge before they attend the university event. During lunch, read works by an author who will soon visit the university. Create a learning center on artistic movements covered in upcoming exhibits. Any fun and educational mini lessons related to the university's program empower students to be informed, active learners on their field trip.

Every field trip is a program opportunity. When you hear announcements about upcoming trips or see them listed on school calendars, ask sponsoring teachers to give a mini program that prepares students for the trip. Often, the best teachers coordinate field trips with lessons they're either beginning or have just finished in the classroom. While students are engaged in classroom learning, you can support their lesson by hosting a program on a related topic. If you're unable to capitalize on any of these opportunities, then at the very least ask teachers to bring back materials from the trip so you can offer them to library patrons. Items may include interactive programs from the science museum, sample demos from the local radio station, or Webographies of art and artists from the fine arts museum.

Even if no one plans a field trip to these facilities, you can bring part of that institution to your campus. A professor of architecture in Chicago not only narrates guided boat tours through downtown, but she also travels to schools with a portfolio containing graphics, blueprints, and photographs of the city's skyscrapers to host programs. Institutions of all types have employees and volunteers willing to come to your campus to guide students through riveting educational experiences.

Business and Industry

To fulfill community service responsibilities, businesses frequently collaborate with area schools to help students learn about different professions; many even form partnerships with area schools. When approached, most companies are pleased to help young people learn about their business or offer resources for programs. They can provide guest speakers, print resources, media software, and even financial support for your events. Such generosity is as much pragmatism as altruism. The success of any business depends on good PR. Supporting schools impresses administrators, school board members (who are usually businesspersons in the community), and parents. Furthermore, by sponsoring school events, their company name becomes recognizable to young consumers. While helping you, they are using one of the most cost-effective forms of advertising.

Most large businesses have huge PR departments whose representatives welcome the opportunity to work with library media specialists. Before contacting any businesses, however, know your district's policies about working with businesses. It is essential to keep abreast of what contracts your district has that restrict doing business with certain competitors. For example, many districts sign contracts with specific copy machine corporations or soft drink vendors that require the schools to use only their products. Such deals often come with multimillion-dollar advances that districts could lose if someone even inadvertently violates the contract. Although PR persons should know whether or not their company has commissioned to do business with your district, they may not. Responsibility for that knowledge lies with you.

Fortunately, your administration offices probably have a list of businesses with which they have good relations. Start with that list to secure guest speakers, financial backers, or valuable program resources. Other library media specialists in your district could also recommend companies that have been supportive, or warn you of companies that have reneged on promises. Finally, ask the counselors which local businesses support the schools by participating in career events. Local businesses that give scholarships to your district's high schools often have long-term visions to help students become successful. That spirit of encouragement often translates into great interactions and generous support for any school in the district willing to pursue financial donations.

Some businesses have programs already prepared for presenting at schools. Figure 4.3 lists a few businesses and the topics they shared.

Business/Company	Program Titles
Bakery	Donuts: The "Hole" Story
Bookstore	Murder, Malice, and Mayhem in Young Adult Mysteries
Car dealership	How Cars are Built
Grocery store	From the Farm to the Shelf
Gym	Muscle Up to Fitness
Radio station	You Can Be a D.J.
Restaurant	What Makes It Taste So Good?

Figure 4.3. Examples of businesses with program titles.

In addition to the businesses depicted in Figure 4.3, other professions also have much to offer your students. Some businesses worth contacting:

Airlines
Architectural firms
Automobile dealers
Banks
Beauty salons
Boat and yacht businesses
Building supply stores
Cable companies
Cinemas
Computer stores
Concert promoters
Dentist's offices
Department stores

Doctor's offices
Drug stores
Electric companies
Ethnic food stores
Gas companies
Interior design firms
Jewelers
Landscaping businesses
Law firms
Limousine services
Marketing companies
Motorcycle shops

Music stores
Musical equipment stores
Pet shops
Police and security companies
Radio stations
Sporting goods stores
Stockbrokers
Telephone companies
Theaters
Video stores
Vitamin and nutrition stores
Whole food stores

Clubs and Organizations

Community clubs and organizations cover an array of topics. Because they often specialize in specific interests, their members may be uniquely qualified to share expertise on subjects related to your program. Special interest clubs and organizations can be far-reaching, especially if they contain many subgroups.

Most sports organizations can be exceptionally great community contacts. First, you might explore a group from a familiar sport; volleyball, skiing, tennis, swimming, and soccer may come to mind immediately. You might also consider special-interest sports including skateboarding, surfing, and even river rafting.

Although at first they may seem difficult to contact or to secure support from, consider major sports organizations also. Securing their support usually requires a personal connection, but don't let that fact discourage you. Many coaches in your district may have either played or worked for these organizations. Someone you know from your own campus or another campus in your district can initiate a perfect contact between you and the organization around which you'd like to host a program.

If you cannot find connections, redirect your search to amateur players and coaches. Many amateurs are passionate about their favorite pastime, and are therefore thrilled to share their knowledge with students. Their experience and zeal make amateur athletes among the most popular and effective program presenters. Keep in mind that many middle-school students relate best to high school or college athletes who play their favorite sports.

Cultural arts organizations frequently promote music, dance, and theater in schools. Performing artists such as dancers, thespians, and musicians thrive on artistic expression, and love the change in venue from a large theater to the more intimate surroundings of a school that often affords interaction with students. Although the arts seem to go in and out of political favor, especially in relation to funding, most artists recognize and appreciate the support they get from educators. As a result, they often have prepared programs they advertise among schools in and around the regions where they're based. Find out what the cultural arts organizations in your area offer, or contact them to customize a program with you or merely support a program you've created yourself. If you're fortunate to live near a large city, contact the symphony, ballet, or other cultural organizations that might send presenters to your school.

Nearly all professions have their own organizations where members grow professionally and personally through meetings, workshops, and social events. Look into organizations related to businesses of particular interest to your local community. Easier still, notice what opportunities exist in your own profession. One visit to the exhibits at state or national library conventions illustrates just how many companies travel to schools to promote reading, teach research skills, or offer on-campus computer training. In one exhibit hall, you have numerous program ideas and opportunities laid out before you.

Be creative in considering the abundant possibilities for program help. Both honorary and social sororities and fraternities may provide tremendous program contributions. Conservation groups may want to share programs related to ecology. Psychiatric organizations may have resources related to mental health (adolescents dealing with depression) or physical ailments (eating disorders). Check the newspapers. Trials bring out organizations for and against major issues. Over the past few years, hot topics like teen smoking, youth violence, and Internet scams attract organizations that might have valuable information to share. For hotly debated topics, your program can give students balanced information and enable them to make informed decisions.

All types of organizations can support programming. Whether they send materials, provide guest experts, or simply connect you with online resources, organizations are worth contacting. (Figure 4.4 lists organizations that frequently support programs for middle schools, along with a sample program title.)

Clubs and Organizations	Program Titles
Bankers' association	Understanding Credit Before You Get It
Historical society	Games People Played
Humane society	For the Life of Your Pet
Musicians' organization	The Sounds of Success (Careers for Future Musicians)
Professional women's organization	Career Trends and Opportunities
Sierra Club	Earth Day Every Day: 101 Ways to Save the Planet
Sports organization	Olympic Dreams
Writer's group	Writing Beyond the Classroom Essay

Figure 4.4 Examples of organizations and clubs with program titles.

In addition to the organizations in Figure 4.4, consider:

> Book clubs
> Cultural arts organizations (theater, symphony, ballet, opera)
> Cultural groups (heritage societies, ethnic groups)
> Fraternities and sororities
> Hobby-related groups
> Medical-related charities and foundations
> Pet clubs
> Political organizations
> Professional organizations
> Retired professionals organizations
> Area sports organizations
> Major sports organizations (NFL, WNBA, MLB)
> Sports clubs (tennis, ski, swim)
> Various special interest organizations and clubs

Government Agencies

National, state, and local government agencies have some of the most dependable and thorough materials and resource people accessible to schools. Besides being tremendously well versed on their subject, their program speakers often have extensive prior experience speaking to school-aged audiences. Further, they can supply dependable, well-documented information (brochures, pamphlets) for your vertical file and reference section. Foreign government agencies also share resources through their consulates and embassies. (Figure 4.5, page 82, highlights some government agencies that support middle school curriculum and program titles.) Addresses and telephone numbers for the government agencies are available in the telephone directory, online telephone listings, and at their individual Internet Web sites. Chapter 6 lists Web site addresses for government agencies, along with detailed information about what each offers.

U.S. Government Agencies	Program Titles
National Aeronautics and Space Administration	Aboard the Space Shuttle
Federal Aviation Agency	Highways in the Sky
U.S. Postal Service	What Happens to Your Letter
U.S. Department of Immigration & Naturalization	Becoming a Citizen
Federal Bureau of Investigation	Invisible Clues: DNA
National Parks Service	Practical Conservation
Department of Public Safety	Defensive Driving
Animal Control	Lost Animals
Fire Department	Volunteers and Careers
Police Department	Scared Straight: One Day Inside a Corrections Facility
Municipal Court	A View from a Judge's Bench
Mayor's Office (or City Manager)	What It Takes to Run Your City
Parks and Recreation Department	What's There for You?

Figure 4.5 Examples of government agencies with program titles.

In addition to the agencies listed in Figure 4.5, explore these other government groups:

Department of Agriculture · · · · · · · · · National Weather Service
Drug Enforcement Administration · · · United States Congress
Foreign Consulates and Embassies · · United States Customs Service
Local Government Agencies · · · · · · · United States Mint
Military Branches of the Armed · · · · United States Supreme Court
Services

Media

Newspapers, television stations, radio stations, and magazines can direct you to great resources. Pay special attention to local newspapers and Sunday supplements, especially sections on "upcoming events," "happenings," or "what's going on in the community." These resources announce presentations by authors, scientists, actors, and sports stars. Movies and live dramatic productions of classics provide potential programming ideas. Often, theaters will announce performances held expressly for students at no cost or for a nominal fee.

Let teachers schedule the field trip while you prepare a related program before or after they see the production. Or, you can develop a similar concept within your school. If you know of a good movie version of a novel required in your school's curriculum, cooperatively develop a program around that novel with the teacher(s) who'll be covering the work. Nowadays, many young adult novels are translated into fine films either released theatrically or expressly for cable or network television. Purchase a copy of the video or DVD from a company that provides legal distribution of films to schools and you can create a program that students find both entertaining and enlightening.

Holidays and Special Events

As you plan your programs, capitalize on holidays and special community events. When generating program ideas for national holidays, incorporate a reading component for added relevance. Offer holiday programs associated with literary classics, including O. Henry's *The Gift of the Magi* at Christmas, Truman Capote's *The Thanksgiving Visitor,* and Edgar Allan Poe's "The Raven" for Halloween. If you don't have these resources in your media center, borrow them through interlibrary loan. Even further, check Web sites about these authors for biographical information and support materials.

If you think your middle-school students may have had their fill of events focusing on major national holidays, consider holidays honoring special people, including Columbus Day or Martin Luther King, Jr. Day, or celebrations that may be unique to your area. For example, Founders Day and Memorial Day in many regions invite you to capitalize on great ideas, resources, and collaborations.

Community events also generate program ideas. Art festivals, rodeos, and the Walk of Historic Homes are all local celebrations that you can support through programming. Besides checking your community's calendar of events, contact event organizers to request materials and guest speakers. Rather than developing an independent event, volunteer to host one portion of a large program created and funded by the community.

Chamber of Commerce

The Chamber of Commerce has abundant information about local events. Each year, the members compile a community calendar listing holidays, meetings, celebrations, festivals, and other happenings. They are among the most informed and diverse resource connections you will find, and they can help at every stage of programming. When searching for a relevant program topic, consider offering a program that coincides with a community event listed on the calendar. If you need help contacting local professionals, they can provide names, telephone numbers, and contact persons for nearby businesses as well as organizations and clubs. If you're also looking for a talented guest speaker, they can connect you to speakers' bureaus with experts on many topics. Develop a positive rapport with the Chamber of Commerce. It is likely to be among your best program resources.

CONCLUSION

Clearly, program support only begins within the confines of your own campus. Beyond it are limitless possibilities for finding resource people and materials. Knowing how many resource possibilities exist is the first step to acquiring the very best resources to enhance your program. With the possibilities before you, you're able to choose the most direct path to securing the resources you want, and thus develop a program that makes the greatest impact on your audiences.

5

How to Gather and Organize Resources

Once you know where to find the best resources for your program, you'll want to develop effective strategies for acquiring them. Through your experience as a library media specialist, you already know how to find and gather certain types of resources, such as books. At some point, you've probably also discovered some of the pitfalls of standard acquisition methods. Who hasn't searched for books in our jobber's catalog or database, requested a title (and perhaps extras to ensure getting something on the topic), only to receive the order with none of those books included. Getting an "On order" or "No longer available" notation can be frustrating when ordering books for the general collection. But when you've ordered them to support a scheduled program, such notations can set back your entire planning process.

The process requires even more expertise when taking into account all the different types of resources included in a program. For example, choosing an outstanding speaker for a program would demand far different skills than finding an appropriate video clip, or ordering an exhibit from a museum.

Communication and organization are the keys to the successful acquisition and effective use of resources. No matter how large your program becomes and how many support people you have contributing to the effort, you have the responsibility of coordinating every step of planning and presentation. Knowing how to gather and then get the most from your human and material resources will give your programs the polish that makes them dynamic and unforgettable.

SELECTING VOLUNTEERS

As you select resources, gather a team of people from the groups closest to your school: parents, students, and teachers. In addition to getting people who can complete easy-to-learn program tasks, you will want volunteer help with knowledge related to curriculum or student interests. To choose volunteers most suited to your program needs, gather data through surveys or questionnaires.

Parents

Some parents of middle-school students continue volunteering with the same time and energy they devoted throughout the elementary school years. Many more, however, are eager to help but cannot make long-term volunteer commitments. In either case, they might be available to speak or help at a single school library media program. As speakers, parents can share professional experiences, leisure activities, travel adventures, or expertise on their favorite topics. Some may give fine demonstrations or make impressive media presentations. At the very least, some parents who are unable to share their time may have materials they're willing to contribute for displays or exhibits.

The easiest way to gather information on parents' interests and expertise is by sending surveys to them at the beginning of the year. First, meet with your principal to request permission to distribute the surveys. Make the most of this meeting by following these simple suggestions:

- Begin by summarizing your plans for school library media programs.

- Describe the need for program resources.

- Explain the reasons for sending the survey.

- Discuss the benefits (to students, faculty members, and you) of using parents as resources.

- Share with your principal a copy of the survey and letter that you will send to parents.

After securing the principal's permission, stress to teachers the far-reaching value of your survey. Explain that you will organize and file the surveys, then make them available for their use. Then ask them to help get the surveys out to parents through the children.

Timing the distribution of these surveys can make a significant difference in the number of responses you receive. If your school distributes student handbooks that include forms that parents must fill out for the administration and the nurse, be sure to have your surveys ready to distribute with the handbooks. If parents receive them all together, they are more likely to complete them all and make sure their child takes the completed forms back to school by the requested deadline.

Because the law requires some forms, especially the health and emergency contact information, parents are usually conscientious about filling them out in a timely manner. If you wait to send out your surveys after the required forms are returned, parents are less likely to be so conscientious, and many surveys will trickle in gradually, or not at all. If you want parents to give them their due consideration, make your surveys seem as important as the emergency forms parents expect to receive at the beginning of every school year. Figure 5.1 illustrates a survey that can be sent to parents.

Dear Parents:

Our school library media center is gathering ideas for special programs to offer as a means of supporting and enriching curriculum. If you have a hobby, special talent, skill, interest, or travel experience that you would like to share, please complete the survey below, and return it to your child's teacher.

Thank you,
Daniel Harmon
Library Media Specialist

Date _____

COMMUNITY RESOURCES QUESTIONNAIRE

_____ Yes, I would like to share information/materials with the students at Barbara Snitkin Middle School.

Name _____ Telephone _____

Name(s) of middle school children   Name(s) of homeroom teacher(s)

_____   _____

_____   _____

Special hobbies/crafts:

Description of hobby/craft:_____

_____

_____ I would be willing to discuss it with students.
_____ I would be willing to demonstrate it.
_____ I would be willing to share it with students as an exhibit.

Special talents/skills:

Description of talent/skill: _____

_____

_____ I would be willing to discuss it with students.
_____ I would be willing to demonstrate it.
_____ I would be willing to contribute materials for a display.
_____ I would be willing to share my storytelling ability with students.

Travel experiences:

Description (places): _____
_____ I would like to discuss it with students.
_____ I have slides, films, or photographs to share with students.
_____ I have interesting materials from this country to contribute to a display.

Figure 5.1. Community resources questionnaire for parents.

Survey results identify parents' specific knowledge, skills, unique possessions, nonprint materials, and hobbies. They also indicate in what capacity each parent is able to volunteer. Regardless of the survey format, request several ways to contact parents. Beyond this requirement, you might further modify the survey to fit the programming needs of your particular facility.

Students

Sometimes, the completed parent surveys may mention a son's or daughter's collections and special hobbies. More often, you will discover students' interests by interacting with them. Even students with little public-speaking experience may have the enthusiasm and knowledge to captivate an audience of their peers. With a little coaching on how to streamline their presentation, students may become primary contributors to your most riveting programs.

**Photo 5.1. Student volunteers assist in fulfilling daily tasks as the
media specialist and volunteers prepare for programs.**
(Harry F. Byrd Middle School, Richmond, Virginia, Henrico County Public Schools)

Teachers

After gathering the survey data, enter all relevant information into a community resources file. (Details for establishing the community resources file appear in the next section.) Then make the file available to teachers. Also, foster a positive rapport with your colleagues by repaying them for helping distribute the surveys. As you learn about teachers' lessons, special projects, and classroom programs, flip through your files to find possible volunteers who might support the teacher with a guest visit or materials to enhance a unit. A brief note or tip about potential parent helpers in the classroom can be invaluable to teachers. Even if you don't have specific recommendations, occasionally remind colleagues that your files are available for their perusal.

Finally, consider teachers as another program resource. Many departments are filled with outstanding teaching materials that enhance programming. Though most teachers are already overworked, some find sharing a special skill and interest rejuvenating. To learn of their interests, give teachers a survey similar to the one in Figure 5.1. Encourage them to record hobbies, collections, travel experiences, and skills they might enjoy presenting to students.

The teachers' survey promises three other benefits. It makes teachers more aware of what the school library media center has to offer their students. It encourages them to look for possible resources to add to the file. It adds teacher recommendations to your list of program resources.

MAKING IT WORK WITH VOLUNTEERS

Recruiting and working with volunteers is essential for programming. Usually, parents help plan, prepare, and present programs. At other times, they fulfill regular media center duties while you and other volunteers work on special programs. Some like to share their skills and talents by volunteering as guest speakers. In any role, they are a valuable resource whose support should not be underestimated.

Parent volunteers can also help you with clerical tasks related to programming, especially developing a community resources file. After you generate a set of questions for potential community resources, allow parent volunteers to make the telephone contacts. Put one or two in charge of recording the information that creates the initial file. Later, others can take over developing and updating the resources file.

Prepare for Volunteers

Before gathering a parent volunteer team, know the district policy on obtaining volunteers. In some districts, policies are open-ended, leaving decisions to campus administrators. Others specify exact requirements such as how many they can recruit, how they can be acquired, and how they should be assessed throughout the year. Whether strict or lenient, most districts have written guidelines about bringing volunteers into the building. In this era of heightened security concerns, following district or campus rules on the matter is essential. In those rare cases where a written policy is not already in place, suggest creating one with the campus site-based committee or the faculty at large.

No matter what the circumstance, secure the principal's permission for whatever you do. It may take a dash of diplomacy and more than one meeting to convince the principal that you even need volunteers. Be persuasive and persistent. Even if you have support staff, volunteers are integral to program success.

After receiving permission to recruit or add more volunteers, keep the principal abreast of every stage of your volunteer program. Share a copy of the Volunteer Form in Figure 5.2 and the Volunteer Task Request in Figure 5.3, page 92. Update the principal on successes you owe to volunteer support. Most important, introduce parent volunteers to the principal (and his or her secretary) when they first begin working, then invite the principal to the library media center occasionally to see how much the volunteers are contributing to the school.

Recruit Volunteers

Simple forms are often the most successful recruiting tools. Succinct, direct requests set a professional tone. Parents who volunteer regularly will respect your efficiency. Though they work for free, they want their volunteer time to be productive. Parents who have never volunteered nor worked in a modern school library media center may be apprehensive. A well-written request form makes a good impression. If the forms alone don't inspire cooperation, then the information they provide may lead to future interactions that will.

CONTACTING RESOURCES

Although you will most likely set your own program goals and make all final decisions about program content, you can delegate many other responsibilities to volunteers. Though not difficult to do, contacting resource people and organizing the contact information are important. Worthwhile programs need good contact people and material resources. Finding them and accessing information about them requires communication and organization skills.

List Possible Resources

Prepare your volunteers to contact possible resources. First, describe your program goals and the resources you think can support it. Then discuss with your volunteers the campus, district, and community resources listed in Chapter 4. Help your volunteers begin their searches. Guide them to references that initiate their searches. District contact lists, local telephone directories, and Internet search engines may all be fine starting points for locating resources. Be available to answer questions or offer help, but trust that your volunteers can handle the task alone. Again, this process is not difficult. It just takes time, persistence, and a little tenacity.

Dear Parents:

Our school library media center needs your help. To keep the media center functioning at maximum potential, we depend on parent volunteers who make it possible to carry out unique activities and programs. Would you be willing to work in the school library media center for several hours per week? If not, could you help us by performing some duties at home? Please complete the following questionnaire if you are interested in volunteering in any capacity. Your consideration is greatly appreciated.

- -

**LIBRARY MEDIA CENTER
VOLUNTEER FORM**

Name _____ Days and times available to work in LMC

Address _____ _____

Phone _____ _____

E-mail _____ _____

Name(s) of middle school child(ren)   Homeroom Teachers

_____   _____

_____   _____

_____   _____

Special skills/talents/interests

_____ Word processing   _____ Artwork/Graphics
_____ Internet research   _____ Laminating
_____ Read aloud   _____ Filing
_____ Storytelling   _____ Book repair

Type of work _____

_____

Figure 5.2 Volunteer recruitment form sent to parents.

VOLUNTEER TASK REQUEST

Volunteer's name _____

Volunteer's telephone _____

Days and times available _____

Please check the library media center tasks that interest you

_____ Word processing
_____ Working at circulation desk
_____ Laminating
_____ Helping to process books
_____ Helping to develop learning centers
_____ Contacting resources and recording information in resource file
_____ Repairing damaged books
_____ Shelving books
_____ Processing audiovisual materials
_____ Maintaining vertical file
_____ Supervising reference area
_____ Assisting with displays and exhibits
_____ Filing cards

Figure 5.3 Volunteer task request form (to be given to volunteers after orientation).

Interview Potential Resources

Once your volunteers have a list of contacts, let them conduct telephone interviews to determine what program support each contact can provide. Recommend that volunteers keep the interview succinct. They should begin by introducing themselves, then explaining that they have called to secure program support. Immediately after, volunteers should ask predetermined questions like those listed below. Whenever possible, have them tailor questions to the goals of a particular program. Also, word the questions so that volunteers can jot down information simply and effectively during the conversation. The more directly your questions are pointed to the exact information you seek, the less time volunteers will have to spend recapping or elaborating on the feedback the potential volunteer offered in conversation.

1. Are you interested in sharing information concerning your field of expertise, skills, or area of interest with middle-school students?

2. Are you willing to visit (or send people from your business) to our school?

3. What would you (or your business) like to offer students?

4. Do you think you can tailor the information to middle-school students?

5. Do you have program material already prepared?

6. What is the length of time needed for the program?

7. What types of information will you share during the presentation?

8. Will you need a computer or audiovisual equipment?

9. Are there certain days that you are available?

10. How much notice do you require to share a prepared presentation?

11. How much notice do you require to develop a presentation for one of our programs?

12. Do you charge a speaking fee?

13. Could you supply any handouts to the students?

14. Would you be able to provide materials for a display or exhibit?

15. Do you know a teacher or parent at this school?

During the interview, volunteers should take notes. If they're following the listed questions systematically, notes they take during the telephone conversation should end up relatively well organized and ready to use.

After asking the predetermined questions, they can request brochures or pamphlets that provide more information. Finally, volunteers should thank the contact person, but leave the final statement open-ended. They may say, "Thank you for your time. I will share this information with the media specialist." Or, "Thank you for sharing this information. You've been very helpful." Be sure volunteers do not state or imply that someone will call back. Even if the contact seems promising, you may find a better, more convenient, or less expensive resource. Or, you may end up changing your program plans. Leave your options open, and do not let volunteers create expectations of you that you may not be able to or want to fulfill.

After their telephone interviews, review the information and, if necessary, discuss that contact person further with your volunteers. Primarily, decide if the information on this contact is worth saving for future use. Based on curricular needs and student interests, is this person or business a good potential resource for future programs? If the answer is yes, then keep the questionnaire in a community resources file, or succinctly record the information onto a community resources card. For easy access, have someone organize the resource files or cards, brochures, and pamphlets.

ORGANIZING THE RESOURCES

After identifying and contacting resources from the community, organize the resources. Use whatever method makes the most sense to you. Volunteers are temporary. In subsequent years, you are the one who will need to find those contact lists, resources, and materials. Create whatever system will enable you to access information quickly and explain the system easily to teachers and future volunteers. Both a community resources file and a vertical file can help.

Establish a Community Resources File

Creating a community resources file for your campus or district is worthwhile for all types of program development, including special programs initiated by teachers and administrators. Place resource data into a separate file drawer organized in whatever way seems most appropriate. You may prefer to arrange all resources alphabetically. Or, it might be more efficient to organize them by the different types of resources identified in Chapter 4. Another logical strategy is to organize resources according to the programs for which you used them. Whatever organizational style works for you, use it consistently and make sure anyone who uses or updates the files knows your method so you can access all resource information as soon as you need it.

Instead of keeping a separate resources file, you may prefer to store resource data with other program materials. For easy access, you might store background information, notes on modifications for next year, student art, and lists of resource people and materials in one file. When you repeat the program, you'll find everything stored in one place.

Share Resources and Responsibilities

Once you've established your file, inform department chairpersons or individual classroom teachers about the location and organization of program resources. Not only will this help them find materials when they plan a unit, but it also enables them to contribute more resources to the library media center when they find something new to add to the file.

Establishing a community resources file for a school seems like an overwhelming task, but it doesn't have to be. After making the commitment to develop such a file, lighten the load by assigning the work to parent volunteers. To start the process, implement the following steps.

Select Interested Parent Volunteers

To establish the file, brainstorm with parent volunteers and teachers. Devise a systematic plan to develop the file. Then recruit volunteers who enjoy projects involving organization and who can see the job through to completion. Usually by discussing the project with volunteers, some will be genuinely interested. It is best to let only one or two volunteers tackle the project; that way, they can better claim ownership of the work. The volunteers can pursue the project in the school library media center once a week. If they need more time, you may suggest they work on the project at home.

Determine the Best Format

Sometimes consistency makes finding resources easy. Consequently, some media specialists organize everything using the exact same format. Others look at the materials they must organize, and determine the easiest way to store it now and access it again in the future. Whatever format you choose, keep it simple. Teachers should be able to search through them without needing your help. The most common formats include:

1. *Folder format.* Folders are arranged alphabetically by topic in a filing cabinet, much like a vertical file. In each folder, store flyers, pamphlets, handouts, and photos, as well as information about the community resources. (See Figure 5.4, page 96, for a community resources sample form.)

2. *Catalog card format.* Record all information on a single, small card, and include a notation about where to find related materials. (See Figure 5.5, page 97.)

3. *Larger card (usually 4 x 6) format.* Record information on the cards arranged in an appropriately sized file box. Store the box near materials associated with the program.

4. *Electronic format.* If you have an online catalog system that uses standard MARC format, you may want to incorporate community resources information into the MARC format designed specifically for community resources. If you do not have an online catalog, you can develop your own community resources database using a database management program.

Determine What the File Should Contain

Regardless of the format you choose, record the following information on each card about every resource:

- Date
- Name of person, business, company, institution, club, agency
- Street and e-mail address
- Fax and telephone number
- Time available
- Length of program
- Special audiovisual equipment needs
- Appropriate target group to which the resource will appeal (age, grade)
- Fees (if any)
- General program description

COMMUNITY RESOURCES FORM

 Topic _____   Date Entered _____

Name _____

Contact person _____

Address _____

_____

Telephone _____ Fax _____

E-mail address _____

Type of program _____

Grade levels _____

Length of time required _____

Equipment needs _____

Availability _____

Fees _____

Program description _____

_____

_____

_____

_____

Comments_____

_____

_____

Figure 5.4. Sample form for community resources file folder.

Topic _____   Date Entered _____

Name _____   Grade levels _____

Address _____   Availability _____

_____   Equipment needs: _____

Telephone _____   _____

Fax _____   Fee _____

E-mail _____

Description

_____

_____

Comments

_____

_____

Figure. 5.5. Sample card for community resources file.

Somewhere on the card, include a brief evaluation of the resource after using it and the date of the evaluation. For example, after a program with a guest speaker, record personal observations and feedback from teachers and students about the speaker on the reverse side of the form or card.

Determine File Arrangement

Arranging the file is important especially if faculty members, staff, and administrators will be using it. Some arrangements to consider:

- Arrange alphabetically by name of person or business
- Arrange alphabetically by topic to which that resource contributes
- Arrange by subject area
- Cross reference by name, topic, and subject area

Determine Who May Use the File

It is best to make the community resources file available to all faculty members at your school, to administrators, other media specialists in the district, and, in some cases, students working on projects. When school library media specialists and the local public library staff work together and share files, patrons of both benefit, and the work of maintaining a file is easier to justify. By sharing, everyone has access to more resources.

Because so few media specialists have a community resources file, some industrious media specialists join together to establish one file to be shared among campuses throughout the district. Thanks to the common practice of interlibrary loan, even students are familiar with the concept of shared resources.

Publicize the Availability of the File

For the file to be used, you must advertise its availability to teachers, the principal, parents, students, and others in the district. Share your rationale for developing the file and remind them that its existence enhances programs in the classroom and throughout the school. Not only will the file help you develop programs, but it also encourages teachers to begin programming as well. Even if they never use the file for anything else, teachers will be grateful to you for providing access to guest speakers.

Revise the File Regularly

Determine a policy for updating the file and add it to the formal school library media center policy manual. Updating the file is necessary. Yet, as most library media specialists know, this task is much like the weeding process. Although the work is not difficult, finding time to do it may be a challenge. Therefore, assign the job of keeping up with the community resources file to one or two volunteers who enjoy this type of work. Let them be responsible for deleting inaccurate or outdated contact information as well as adding new or updated data. Simply verifying the information every year or two will ensure easy contacts when you need them.

CONCLUSION

Once you know how to find, gather, and organize resources, you're well equipped to put together truly dynamic programs. Knowing about resources within and beyond the community can support programming in the most vital way. That knowledge is a tool that transforms ordinary, predictable programs into riveting events rich in content and extended learning.

6

Searching the Internet for Resources

Just as the Internet has become an integral part of nearly all research assignments for students, it is also an invaluable source of information for you as a media specialist. No matter how extensive and thorough your reference section, your periodical and book collection, and even your professional network may be, the Internet still contains voluminous information that can be accessed literally in seconds. At this time, the primary concern of educators is distinguishing which Web sites present reliable information.

To address that concern in relation to programming, this chapter contains a handy list, with descriptions, of some of the best Internet sites for educators, especially those that can support library programming.

This chapter includes Web sites in three general categories and several subcategories that all support and enrich library programs. They are:

1. **Resources to Support Curriculum**

> Businesses and Industry
>
> Government Agencies
>
> Institutions (aquariums, libraries, museums, universities, zoos)
>
> Virtual Field Trips
>
> Young Adult Literature

2. **Resources to Support Youth Interests**

> All-Around Resources
>
> Colleges and Careers
>
> Entertainment
>
> Magazine Web Sites Designed Especially for Students
>
> Newspapers and Magazines
>
> Sports

3. **Resources to Support Media Specialists and Teachers**

Copyright

Curriculum

General Resources

Professional Associations

Professional Journals

Special Middle School Sites

The Web sites related to curriculum listed at the beginning of the chapter correspond to the community resources highlighted in Chapter 4. Sites pertaining to authors of young adult literature can also be found in the curriculum section. Other Web sites provided in this chapter relate to middle-school curriculum, youth interests, and resources for media specialists and teachers. Some sites were created expressly for educators. Others include pages specifically designed for teens. Every Web site contains valuable information for media specialists, teachers, and middle-school students.

Sites indicated with an asterisk [*] offer excellent starting points, as they provide links to numerous other resources related to the specific category. All the sites listed support programming in the following ways:

- You may gather ideas to plan and develop programs.

- You may gain more information on the program topic.

- You may use them to locate resources, including people, exhibits, activities, pamphlets, and other supplemental resources.

- Teachers may acquire information and activities to prepare students for upcoming programs.

- Students may access the Web sites to research a program topic, participate in on-line activities, or take virtual field trips to extend and reinforce learning.

- Educators may use them to extend library programs through follow-up activities for students.

RESOURCES TO SUPPORT
THE CURRICULUM

Many of the Web sites listed in this chapter were created expressly for students and teachers to use as educational tools. All of the areas, particularly the English/Language Arts and author section, have obvious connections to school library media center programming. Web sites with a more general interest base can meaningfully serve the same purpose. Businesses and government agencies support math, science, and social studies. Institutions enhance programs in those core curriculum areas, as well as in electives. They prove especially relevant for fine arts classes, as museums in particular develop many educational resources (often for free) to support educational programs. As you explore these possibilities, note that we chose all Web sites because their strong content offers direct support to curriculum.

Business and Industry

Web sites for businesses and corporations abound. Knowing where to find listings of businesses within your community and across the United States can speed your planning stages considerably. In addition to providing extensive information, businesses and corporations are excellent resources for finding guest speakers, supplemental material, and even financial support for programming.

Super Pages
http://www.superpages.com
>This site lists businesses by category or state and has educational links to reference sources and resources for teachers.

Guide to the Web
http://www.theactgroup.com/webguide_directories.htm
>This extensive site contains the following sections that will provide media specialists access to various resources:

- Switchboard—nationwide telephone and address directory
- InfoSpace—personal, business, and government phone, fax and e-mail
- Anywho—fast, clear directory also includes a reverse directory
- SuperPages.com—national business yellow pages and residential listings from NYNEX
- WhoWhere—an e-mail address database
- Zip Code and Zip + 4 Finder—a simple and efficient zip code directory

* *Smartpages.com*
http://http1.smartpages.com/
>This online directory of business listings and city and shopping guides is designed to help consumers shop; research products and services; locate merchants; and plan entertainment, leisure, and travel activities.

Government Agencies

Many government agencies have Web sites that can enrich library programs. Some sites include pages specifically designed for educators. Access these sites to research a program topic, develop program ideas, gather resources, and plan activities.

Some of these sites have gradually added components directed to students. As a result, you might also encourage students to visit some sites before or after attending your program to learn more about the topic. Students will enjoy learning about the topic and participating in the entertaining activities. Also note that many government sites include areas for teachers and parents. Some contain virtual tours and online libraries that provide maps, photographs, and other helpful resources.

Access America for Students: Student Gateway to the U.S. Government
http://www.students.gov

> Users can access this site 24 hours a day for online information and services. Services offered include registering to vote, registering for the selective service, applying for federal financial aid, searching for a job, filing taxes, changing addresses, and much more. The site also lists other government links.

Air Force
http://www.af.mil/

> The online gallery offers photographs and detailed information about topics such as U.S. Air Force operations, careers, and aircraft. Portraits and information about current and past leaders is also available. The section that highlights the active and retired aircraft is a favorite of middle-school students. (The other branches of the military also offer their own sites.)

**Ben's Guide to U.S. Government for Kids*
http://bensguide.gpo.gov/

> The U.S. Government Printing Office developed this site as a guide to information and Web sites about the government. It includes historical documents, branches of the government, and the election process. The site is organized by grade ranges (K–2, 3–5, 6–8, 9–12) and includes an area for parents and teachers. The site's best feature is its extensive listing of government Web sites organized by subject area, making it an excellent starting point for exploring the government on the Internet.

Central Intelligence Agency (CIA)
http://www.odci.gov/cia/ciakids/

> This interactive and fun-filled site explains the functions and background of the CIA. It also offers a virtual tour of the CIA. Students will particularly enjoy the "CIA Canine Corp," "Try a Disguise," and the "CIA Exhibit Center."

CongressLink
http://www.congresslink.org/

> The CongressLink site is presented by the Dirksen Congressional Center, "a non-profit, nonpartisan research and educational organization." The home page includes the "Congressional Information Center" where users can enter a zip code and find their Congress member's address, search Congress, find local media organizations, search for bills and voting records, and find Congressional schedules. The site also includes links to Web sites and lesson plans on subjects such as the Constitution, Congress, the veto process, and the election process.

Department of Health and Human Services
http://www.hhs.gov/

    This site provides useful links to numerous others that contain information about different agencies in the federal government. All of these sites, some of which are listed individually in this chapter, focus on teaching children about the agencies through activities and games.

Federal Bureau of Investigation (FBI) for Kids and Youth
http://www.fbi.gov/kids/kids.htm

    Students learn much about the FBI at this site, which is divided into three visitor levels: kids (K–5), youth (6–12), and parent/teacher. A special Department of Justice (DOJ) page teaches forensics, DNA testing, polygraph testing, and fingerprinting. In areas such as "Working Dogs," "Crime Detection," and "Crime Prevention," students learn about the various departments of the FBI. The "Most Wanted" and "Major Investigations" sections are especially popular with middle-school students. An extensive library arranged by topic offers a multitude of information about crime. Career information is also provided at this interesting site.

Federal Emergency Management Agency (FEMA)
http://www.fema.gov/

    Here, students can learn about the different types of disasters, including tornadoes, earthquakes, and hurricanes. In addition to general weather information, this site teaches safety tips, including a section that helps families prepare for disaster.

The Federal Web Locator
http://www.infoctr.edu/fwl/

    The Center for Information Law and Policy provides this service as "the one-stop shopping point for federal information on the World Wide Web." For quick searching, the site organizes the links by federal agency areas, or users can view the complete contents of the site. The site offers an extensive listing of links and states "maintained to bring the cyber citizen to the federal government's doorstep."

Louisiana State University. "A List of Federal Agencies on the Internet"
http://www.lib.lsu.edu/gov/exec.html

    This site lists all the U.S. federal government agencies on the Internet and links them to their sites. It has two main divisions: "Executive Branch and Agencies," and "Independent Establishments and Government Corporations." Subheadings for each division are the same and include "Judicial"; "Legislative"; "Independent"; "Boards, Commissions, and Committees"; "Quasi-Official"; and "Complete U.S. Federal Government Agencies Directory."

National Aeronautics and Space Administration (NASA) Education Program
http://education.nasa.gov/

    Linked to *A Guide to NASA's Education Programs,* this searchable database contains brief descriptions of NASA's education programs, including points of contact, admission criteria, location, content areas, and financial support for all of NASA's field centers. Visitors can access a variety of educational programs, materials, and services.

Here you will find contact information and resources arranged by NASA field centers, states, and regions throughout the United States.

National Archives and Records Administration. "The Digital Classroom"
http://www.nara.gov/education/classrm.html

To encourage teachers at all levels to use archival documents in the classroom, the "Digital Classroom" shares materials from the National Archives and methods for teaching with primary sources.

*National Park Service
http://www.nps.gov/

This central hub for almost all of the 375 sites found in the National Park System connects educators to numerous sites focusing on "America's natural and cultural heritage through the National Parks." The Web pages listed range from publications, video presentations, and guided walks and talks, to extensive curriculum-based education programs.

U.S. Department of Energy Office of Science
http://www.science.doe.gov/

When visiting this site, students and educators will learn about science, technology, energy, engineering, and math. Interesting and fun-filled activities enrich the learning experience.

U.S. Department of Treasury
http://www.ustreas.gov/education.html

Students can find information on topics such as U.S. coins, paper money, and our national bank system. The "Treasury's Learning Vault" focuses on topics such as the history of our Treasury and provides a library packed with related resources. A favorite area is the "U.S Mint," which shares basic information about how money is minted.

White House
http://www.whitehouse.gov/

Take an online tour of the White House and meet the president and first lady. Learn about its history and tour its art gallery. The "Gateway to Government" provides links to the president's cabinet. Viewers are encouraged to send mail to the president, vice president, and their spouses.

Institutions

Because many institutions are directly linked to education, they are among the best resources to support programming. Rather than sharing only general information, many of these Web sites offer activities for students, interactive games, teacher resources, online libraries, and virtual tours of exhibits and galleries. When planning your program, take advantage of the extensive information most of these sites share on a variety of topics. They can provide many things, including guest speakers and exhibits, to support science, math, social studies, and the arts.

Aquariums

National Aquarium in Baltimore
http://www.aqua.org/

Visitors are invited to dive into this Web site of fun information about animals, exhibits, conservation efforts, and the institution itself. "Aquarium Fact Sheets," "College Internship Opportunities," and a teachers' section will be of interest to students and educators.

UnderWater World
http://www.underwaterworld.com/

Visit UnderWater World at the Mall of America in Bloomington, Minnesota, and you can take a trip not only through, but also under the aquarium's exhibits: a Minnesota Lake, the Mississippi River, the Gulf of Mexico, and a Caribbean reef.

University of Hawaii. "The Waikiki Aquarium."
http://www.mic.hawaii.edu/aquarium/

This outstanding site offers a beautiful virtual tour where users can click on any creature to gain information about it. The library area provides a searchable database of Web sites and resources about the aquarium, its exhibits, and Hawaiian and South Pacific marine life.

Libraries

George Bush Presidential Library and Museum
http://bushlibrary.tamu.edu/

When using the Internet for program enrichment, don't forget about the wealth of information that can be found at the presidential libraries. This site offers biographies, research, a tour of the museum, and educational opportunities.

Herbert Hoover Presidential Library and Museum
http://www.hoover.nara.gov/

Many other presidential libraries offer original and diverse approaches to sharing information. Some, such as this one on Hoover, focus on more than just the presidential years, and covers the president's entire life and accomplishments.

Library of Congress
http://lcweb.loc.gov/

Browse this huge site to become familiar with the plethora of information available to support media center programs. Overviews of the Library of Congress exhibitions are shared at the online gallery. The "Fun Site for Kids and Family" offers a variety of learning experiences for youngsters and teens. For example, "Meet Amazing Americans" presents photographs and detailed information about famous inventors, politicians, performers, and activists.

New York Public Library
http://www.nypl.org/
>This site has everything imaginable for library users: catalogs, a digital library collection, archival collections, health information, and electronic resources. "Teen Link" provides recommended book lists and links teens to categories such as fun, sports, and homework help. "TV & Movies" is a popular spot for teens.

*School Libraries on the Web
http://www.sldirectory.com/
>This site lists library Web pages maintained by school libraries in the United States and in countries around the world. It includes all grades K–12.

*Virtual YA Index: Public Libraries with Young Adult Web Pages
http://www.suffolk.lib.ny.us/youth/virtual.html
>This site lists public library Web pages with young adult areas.

*Web66
http://web66.coled.umn.edu/
>Web66 maintains the Internet's oldest and most complete list of school Web servers.

Museums

*Kids World 2000: Museums Around the World
http://now2000.com/kids/museums.shtml
>Visit this site for links to all types of museums throughout the world.

*MuseumStuff.com
http://www.museumstuff.com/
>"Welcome to the World of Museums Online" opens this site that offers thousands of museum-related Web sites. Users can search for a museum or exhibit by type or location, play fun games, visit the museum shops, or send e-cards. The "featured virtual exhibits" are organized by subjects and include a wide variety of interesting virtual tours such as "Native American," "Dinosaurs," or "Natural History." The site also lists more than 8,127 other museum-related links.

The Smithsonian Institution
http://www.si.edu/
>This address takes you to the home page of the Smithsonian Institution with links to its "Education and Outreach," "The Virtual Smithsonian," "Online Collections," and much more. The "Education and Outreach" area offers links to a variety of teacher resources including "Museum Studies," "Encyclopedia Smithsonian," and "Resources for Teachers."

Air and Space

The International Women's Air and Space Museum
http://www.iwasm.org/

   Like the museum now located at Burke Lakefront Airport in Dayton, Ohio, this site is dedicated to "preserving the history of women in aviation." Biographical information, photographs, and interesting facts about women who have made major contributions to aviation and space are available.

National Air and Space Museum
http://www.nasm.si.edu/nasm/edu/

   This site contains information and activities about aviation and space topics such as the exploration of the universe. Be sure to explore the educational links, the online galleries, and the special area for teachers.

Art

Yahooligans: Arts and Entertainment: Art: Museums and Galleries
http://www.yahooligans.com/Arts_and_Entertainment/Art/Museums_and_Galleries/

   This excellent site links visitors to more than 75 different museums and galleries including the Smithsonian, the Guggenheim, and the Library of Congress: American Treasures. The listing is alphabetical and includes a brief description of the museum or gallery. Some of the outstanding art museum sites that can be accessed include:

- *Fine Arts Museum of San Francisco.* **http://www.thinker.org/**

- *Louvre Museum.* **http://www.louvre.fr/louvrea.htm**

- *The Metropolitan Museum of Art.* **http://www.metmuseum.org/**

- *National Gallery of Art.* **http://www.nga.gov/**

- *Smithsonian Institution: National Museum of American Art.*
  http://www.nmaa.si.edu/

   Visitors to the above sites will discover virtual tours of galleries, in-depth looks at specific artists and works of art, and virtual tours of current or past exhibits. Many of these sites list services for teachers and schools, teaching resources, and information to use when visiting the galleries.

History

National Museum of the American Indian
http://www.si.edu/nmai/

   The museum, located in Washington, D.C., highlights American Indian history. The Web site provides detailed information concerning the various programs offered.

Smithsonian. *"National Museum of American History"*
   http://americanhistory.si.edu/
   The well-designed virtual exhibitions include a variety of topics such as "The American Presidency" and "Star-Spangled Banner." This site offers a plethora of information to enrich American history projects as well as library programs related to American history.

Science

American Museum of Natural History
   http://www.amnh.org/
   One of the world's finest museums located in New York City can be accessed online. You don't want to miss the virtual tours (complete with sound) of the museum's various exhibits. Be sure to browse the online version of the museum's popular journal, *Natural History.*

Franklin Institute
   http://sln.fi.edu/
   Take an online journey and learn about science topics and exhibits at this Philadelphia museum. Science educators and media specialists planning a science-related program will find links to Internet resources, games, puzzles, science activities, and lessons.

Museum of Science: Boston
   http://www.mos.org/
   Viewers of this site can visit excellent online exhibits. For example, "The Virtual Fish Tank" turns your computer into an aquarium. Various activities, resources, and Web links make this an excellent resource for enriching science programs.

The Museum of Science, Art, and Human Perception (San Francisco).
"The Exploratorium"
   http://www.exploratorium.edu/
   Housed in San Francisco's Palace of Fine Arts, the Exploratorium is a "collage of 650 science, art, and human perception exhibits." These exhibits are highlighted at this site, and a digital index to 10,000 pages of the Exploratorium Web site provides information on a vast array of topics.

Smithsonian Institution. "National Museum of Natural History"
   http://www.mnh.si.edu/
   This is another fine individual site developed by the Smithsonian Institution. The numerous topics highlighted at this site are packed with interesting information and photographs. Electronic field trips, educational resources, and exhibits make this site a top priority when developing library programs.

Universities, Colleges, and Schools

(See also Colleges and Careers under Youth Interests)

*All About College
http://www.allaboutcollege.com/

At *All About College* you'll find thousands of links to colleges and universities around the world, including e-mail addresses for admissions offices for most schools. The list includes colleges in the United States, Canada, Africa, Asia, Europe, Australia, Mexico, and South America. Students can visit the site to locate information about financial aid and to chat with other students.

*American School Directory
http://www.asd.com/

Want to see what's going on at other schools across the nation? Here you can access more than 70,000 school sites. By visiting the individual school sites, library media specialists can gain a wealth of exciting ideas related to special events, curriculum, and activities.

*American Universities and Colleges
http://www.globalcomputing.com/universy.html

This site provides a complete listing of universities and colleges that can be accessed by the name of the college or the state.

Zoos

Bronx Zoo
http://www.bronxzoo.com/

New York's Bronx Zoo is home to more than 4,000 animals, including some of the world's most endangered species. Be sure to take an online tour of the zoo. For example, students won't want to miss the "Congo Virtual Tour," where they meet Congolese residents and play a Congo game.

*Conservation Breeding Specialist Group: Global Zoo Directory
http://www.cbsg.org/gzd.htm

This comprehensive directory of zoos around the world provides links to various sites and information on the nature of each institution's collection.

*Kids World 2000: Animals, Zoos, & Aquariums
http://now2000.com/kids/zoos.shtml

Web site provides "A Guide for the Young Cyber-Traveler" to explore museums, zoos, and aquariums in the United States and around the world. Links are provided for more than 100 museums and more than 50 zoos and aquariums.

London Zoo
http://www.zsl.org/londonzoo/

Established in 1828 and open to the public since 1847, the London Zoo has long been one of the most famous zoos in the world. Visit this site and take a guided tour through the zoo, gather activities, and learn the latest news about the animal residents.

San Diego Zoo
http://www.sandiegozoo.org/

This interactive and information-packed site is a must. Learn facts about animals and zoos as you visit such spots as the "Virtual Photo Album." Photographs, videos, and interactive activities make this an excellent site for enriching library programs.

Smithsonian Institution. "National Zoo"
http://www.si.edu/natzoo/

At this Smithsonian Institution site, see the animals up close with the zoo's "Wild Webcams." On "ZooTV" you can see elephants, flamingos, kiwis, and more. The animal video library allows an online view of the zoo's exhibits.

Virtual Field Trips

Although many sites previously listed include virtual field trips, a few more deserve mentioning. These Web sites prepare students for upcoming programs or reinforce learning afterward. Nearly every site includes special activities worth exploring.

GOALS - Global Online Adventure Learning Site, Inc.
http://www.goals.com/homebody.asp

GOALS provides educational adventures in science, technology, and nature. Adventures include a family voyage aboard a sailboat in the Pacific, a world tour using only human power, and a voyage to circumnavigate the world using oar power.

Is the Tour Better in Person?
http://school.discovery.com/schrockguide/evaltour.html

As students, teachers, and librarians explore the Internet, it is so important to evaluate sites for future use. This evaluation is even more important for virtual tours as these "trips" can enhance learning and create opportunities for students to explore subjects with hands-on experiences. At the site *Kathy Schrock's Guide for Educators*, Kathy Schrock has developed an evaluation criteria page to be used with these virtual tours titled, "Is the Tour Better in Person?" As with all World Wide Web sites, users should evaluate the information and decide if the site is worthwhile and useful.

Passport to Knowledge
http://www.passporttoknowledge.com/

This outstanding site, supported by organizations such as the National Science Foundation, NASA, and public television, contains "interactive learning experiences using space-age telecommunications to connect students and teachers with our planet's leading researchers." The site encourages educators to move beyond the textbook and excite students about science by providing such activities as "Passport to Antarctica" and "Passport to the Rainforest." Online discussion groups, teacher support groups, and teacher resources are also provided.

PostcardsFrom.com
http://www.postcardsfrom.com/

"Hitch a ride in our 'virtual backseat' as we travel America in our RV" begins this site of information and photographs about the United States. The authors, a photographer and graphic designer and a former American history teacher, travel the United States and develop information pages posted to the Web site. Each page shows a "postcard" from the state with links to "Stamps," "Fun Facts," "Artifacts," "Maps," and "Travel Tips." The site is an excellent tool for researching state information such as the state bird, flower, tree, capital, population, and motto. The authors visit one state per week and thus far have visited states from Maine to Texas, from Wisconsin to Hawaii, and many, many more. There is also a "Just for Teachers" area.

Rice University's Virtual Tour: "Glacier"
http://www.glacier.rice.edu/

Rice University sponsors this virtual visit to Antarctica developed by a graduate student, a polar explorer, and a high school teacher with goals to create a Web site and develop "hands-on, inquiry-based, thematic curriculum" for teachers and students. The site provides information and photographs of the region and its inhabitants.

The Virtual Field Trips Site
http://www.field-guides.com/

The virtual trips at this site are really tours through different Web sites to learn about subjects like deserts, hurricanes, oceans, and volcanoes. Each field trip includes detailed lesson plans with terms and concepts to learn before the trip and other ideas, resources, and tools for the teacher and classroom.

Virtual Zoo
http://library.thinkquest.org/11922/

Designed by a high-school Think Quest team, the Virtual Zoo is "a powerful educational tool which serves to heighten the general public's awareness of animals throughout the world." Viewers can visit animals from amphibians to birds to primates to small mammals. Each area includes a description of the animal, pictures, and animal sounds. The site also includes information by habitats with descriptions of the habitat and a listing of the animals found there.

*Yahoo! Recreation: Travel: Virtual Field Trips
http://dir.yahoo.com/recreation/travel/

This site provides links to more than 20 virtual field trips including a bike journey in Africa, an archaeological excavation in Egypt, and Arctic adventures in Greenland. Because of the variety of this listing, it is an excellent place to begin researching virtual tours and journeys.

Young Adult Literature

YA literature is more popular than ever. By tackling more diverse topics, the authors are garnering credibility among and interest from young readers as never before. No longer that vague genre between children's and adult literature, YA books and their authors have much to offer middle-school programs, as indicated by the following list of diverse Web sites.

Books, Reviews, and Awards

ALA Resources for Parents, Teens, and Kids
http://www.ala.org/parents

In the section designated expressly for them, teens can search specific pages such as "Book Lists from the Young Adult Library Service Association" and the "Michael L. Printz Award for Literary Excellence in Literature for Young Adults." For more extensive searches, they can explore the vast offerings from "Book Lists from the Young Adult Library Service Association" and the even more general "TEEN Hoopla: Internet Guide for Teens."

The ALAN Review
http://scholar.lib.vt.edu/ejournals/ALAN/alan-review.html

In each issue, this journal from the National Council of the Teachers of English includes "Clip and File YA Book Reviews." Recently published young adult books are reviewed and include the bibliographic information and a short summary with the review.

*Children's Book Awards
http://www.ucalgary.ca/~dkbrown/awards.html

This section of the Web site, "The Children's Literature Web Guide," is "the most comprehensive guide to English-language children's book awards on the Internet." Although the site has not been updated for some time, it still offers links to many updated award sites. The "United States Awards" area lists all of the ALA awards as well as many others including the *Orbis Pictus Award for Outstanding Nonfiction for Children,* the *Scott O'Dell Award for Historical Fiction,* and the *Boston Globe-Horn Book Award.*

Children's Literature Awards
http://www.norweld.lib.oh.us/ys/awards.htm

Sue McCleaf Nespeca of Youth Services, NORWELD, compiled this wonderful listing of "web sites for various awards or prizes that are granted to children's literature titles." Each award listing includes a description of the award itself and a brief annotation about the Web site. All of the ALA awards are listed as well as the *Boston Globe-Horn Book Awards,* the *School Library Journal's Best Books of the Year, Notable Social Studies Books for Young People,* and many more.

Index to Internet Sites: Children's and Young Adult Authors & Illustrators
http://falcon.jmu.edu/~ramseyil/biochildhome.htm
> This Internet School Library Media Center's section offers an index to author and illustrator sites. Besides the indexed sites, there are links to print bibliographies, author birthdays, interviews online, and author/illustrator appearances. The index is organized alphabetically and is very user friendly.

Kay Vandergrift's Young Adult Literature Page
http://www.scils.rutgers.edu/~kvander/
> Kay Vandergrift's site shares ideas and information about young adult literature and authors. It includes a discussion of the various issues concerning this type of literature. Information about awards and review sources is provided as well as links to bibliographies of authors' works. A unique feature of the site is the video listing (including author videos) and CD-ROMs that support young adult literature.

Winning Titles (YALSA)
http://www.ala.org/yalsa/booklists/
> YALSA (Young Adult Library Services Association) created this site devoted to literature awards and lists specifically for young adults. The sections include "information on the award or list, a nomination form (when available), and links to current and previous winners or lists of titles." Some of the sections are: "Outstanding Books for the College Bound," "Popular Paperbacks," "Quick Picks for Reluctant Young Adult Readers," "Selected Audio Books," and "Selected Videos and DVDs."

Photo 6.1. Popular YA author Will Hobbs autographs books for young fans following another successful program. *(Sedgwick Middle School, West Hartford, Connecticut, West Hartford Public Schools)* **Photo by Phil Zimmerman.**

YA Literature
http://yahelp.suffolk.lib.ny.us/yalit.html
This section of the *Young Adult Librarian's Help/Homepage* offers a variety of links for teens. There is a "Booklists" area as well as "Popular YA Magazines" and "Comics and Graphic Novels." The site has links to other young adult literature areas including Kay Vandergrift's excellent site mentioned above.

Young Adult Authors: Comprehensive Sites

Listed below is a sampling of the Web sites that provide information about the most popular YA authors. There are many sites, and these are just a few of the ones we recommend. Some of the addresses lead you to publisher sites. Others take you to the author's personal Web site. The Web sites for YA authors can be found easily by accessing the sites with an asterisk (*) listed within this section or by visiting the site of the author's publisher. For example, the Kay Vandergrift site listed below not only offers a photograph of the author, biography, bibliography, awards, address, and book reviews with summaries, but also goes one step further and offers links to Web sites.

Biographical information about each author is usually available at the individual author sites. You will also find information about the author's works, including a complete bibliography and a list of awards. At many sites, a photograph of the author, ways to contact him or her, and frequently asked questions are provided. Some sites include links to interviews with the authors.

*Author Bios
http://www2.scholastic.com/teachers/authorsandbooks/authorsandbooks.jhtml
This Scholastic site offers biographies of a variety of authors including YA favorites like Robert Cormier and S.E. Hinton. Each biography shares very personal information directly from the author with birthday, current city of residence, and a listing of awards. Users can then link to the author's book list.

*Index to Internet Sites: Children's and Young Adult Authors & Illustrators
http://falcon.jmu.edu/~ramseyil/biochildhome.htm
This Internet School Library Media Center's section offers an index to author and illustrator sites where biographical information about authors can be found. Besides the indexed sites, there are links to bibliographies, author birthdays, online interviews, and author/illustrator appearances. The index is organized alphabetically and is very user friendly.

*Kay Vandergrift's Young Adult Literature Page
http://www.scils.rutgers.edu/~kvander/
The "Learning About the Author and Illustrator" pages offer a comprehensive listing of more than 600 links to authors and illustrators. Students, teachers, and media specialists who are searching for information about the works and lives of YA authors are almost certain to find links here.

Mystery Writers
  http://www.mysterywriters.net/
    The Mystery Writers of America is the major organization for mystery writers
and other professionals in the field of mystery. The site lists links to more than 75 MWA
authors' sites, many of whose works are enjoyed by middle school students. (*Note:* A
special library program on "Mystery Books" was a real hit in Texas.)

Young Adult Authors: Individual Sites

    The following is just a small sample of popular YA authors. Some have several Web
sites that include biographical information and lists of their works. For your favorite authors
who are not listed below, please visit the recommended sites above that are indicated with
an asterisk.

Avi
  http://www.avi-writer.com/

Bruce Brooks
  http://www.scils.rutgers.edu/~kvander/brooks.html

Caroline Cooney
  http://www2.scholastic.com/teachers/authorsandbooks/authorstudies/jhtml

Robert Cormier
  http://www.randomhouse.com/teachers/authors/corm.html

Sharon Creech
  http://www.sharoncreech.com/

Chris Crutcher
  http://falcon.jmu.edu/~ramseyil/crutcher.htm

Christopher Paul Curtis
  http://www.randomhouse.com/teachers/authors/curtis.html

Karen Cushman
  http://ipl.org/youth/AskAuthor/cushmanbio.html

Lois Duncan
  http://www.iag.net/ˆbarq/lois.html

Karen Hesse
  http://falcon.jmu.edu/~ramseyil/hesse.htm

S. E. Hinton
  http://falcon.jmu.edu/~ramseyil/hinton.htm

Madeline L'Engle
  http://www.randomhouse.com/teachers/authors/leng.html

Lois Lowry
  http://www.ipl.org/youth/AskAuthor/Lowry.html

Walter Dean Myers
    http://aalbc.com/authors/walter/htm

Joan Lowery Nixon
    http://www2.scholastic.com/teachers/authorsandbooks/authorsandbooks.jhtml

Katherine Paterson
    http://www.carolhurst.com/newsletters/31dnewsletters.html

Gary Paulsen
    http://www.randomhouse.com/features/garypaulsen/

Richard Peck
    http://teacher.scholastic.com/authorsandbooks/authorsandbooks.jhtml

J. K. Rowling
    http://www.scholastic.com/harrypotter/author/

Louis Sachar
    http://falcon.jmu.edu/~ramseyil/sachar.htm

Cynthia Voigt
    http://teacher.scholastic.com/authorsandbooks/authorsandbooks.jhtml

RESOURCES TO
SUPPORT YOUTH INTERESTS

To increase patronage and book circulation, school library media specialists often create programs around student interests. Understandably, programs on these themes are usually very successful in reshaping young patrons' attitudes about the media center and about reading. Because so many possibilities exist for programs with student interest themes, it would be impossible to include Web sites to address them all. Instead, we highlight major interests that could apply to a large cross section of your student population, including sports, games, music, movies, and hobbies. Because many middle schools are now encouraging their students to start thinking about college and careers, we have also included great Web sites on those topics as well.

All-Around Resources

*Cool School: The Best Sites on the Web for Teens and Teachers
    http://www.coolschool.edu/
        Vassar College developed this site devoted to young adult students and their teachers. Users can explore specific subject areas like art, music, physics, or literature or "Hang Out" with information on entertainment, sports, magazines, and more. The site also includes college information with a college search, SAT preparation, and even links to college and university home pages. Teachers can visit the "Teacher's Lounge" to check out both general and subject specific resources.

*Internet Public Library Teen Division
http://www.ipl.org/teen/
> Using student advisors and librarians, this Internet Public Library site offers a variety of links for the teen user. Topics include arts and entertainment, clubs and organizations, dating, health, sports, and much more. Each of these sections includes a listing of general resource links with a brief description of the link and the topics covered.

*Teen Hoopla: An Internet Guide for Teens
http://www.ala.org/teenhoopla/
> The Young Adult Library Services Association of ALA created this site to share information of teen interest. Users can read the book reviews written by teens, for teens; explore the "Say What" area where teens can participate in forums such as dress code, teen driving, and violence; or search the links to other teen sites.

Colleges and Careers

For more Web sites related to this category also refer to "Institutions" in the above section.

Internet Public Library—Career and College
http://www.ipl.org/teen/
> Visitors to the Internet Public Library can find career and college information in the teen section that offers links to the following: "Applying for Jobs," "Financial Aid," "Guides to Careers," "Guides to Colleges and Universities," and "Test Preparation." The site also lists a variety of general resource links such as the "Princeton Review Online" and "College and Career Guide for Deaf Students."

Mapping Your Future
http://www.mapping-your-future.org/
> This Federal Family Education Loan Program (FFELP) site gives information to plan a career, choose a school, and pay for the education. Users can take "Guided Tours" and learn what steps to take at every grade level to plan the future.

Peterson's
http://www.petersons.com/
> This information-packed site brings together, at one central address, information about educational opportunities at all levels. It also gives individuals the opportunity to search Peterson's databases, as well as to request more information, and apply to a school or program. Each college, university, and private school has its own site in *Petersons.com.*

Think College
http://www.ed.gov/thinkcollege/
> This U.S. Department of Education site promotes, "Learn for a Lifetime!" Information about educational opportunities beyond high school is presented to three different audiences: "Think College Early" for middle school students, teachers, and parents; "High School and Beyond" for high school and college students; and "Returning to

School" for adult learners. Besides offering excellent information about colleges, financial aid, and career exploration, the site also includes an interactive handbook for middle-school students: "Think College? Me? Now?"

Entertainment

Amusement and Theme Parks

Yahooligans: Listing of Amusement and Theme Parks with Web Sites
http://www.yahooligans.com/Sports_and_Recreation/Amusement_and_Theme_Parks/
> Disney Parks, Six Flags, and Legoland are just a few examples of the sites listed at this useful Web site.

Fun and Games

Calvin & Hobbes
http://www.ucomics.com/calvinandhobbes
> *Calvin & Hobbes* fans can meet Bill Walters, see past strips, meet the characters, and even purchase merchandise.

Haring Kids
http://www.haringkids.com/
> The artist Keith Haring hosts this official site of his work. He offers fun activities for users including an interactive coloring book, art activities, and even lesson plans for teachers.

Hershey's Kidztown
http://www.kidztown.com/
> This site from Hershey's offers fun and games, recipes, the history of the company, and much more!

History of Toys and Games
http://www.historychannel.com/exhibits/toys/
> Users can find the origins of favorite toys and games at this History Channel site and information about successful toy inventors.

Monopoly
http://www.monopoly.com/
> Monopoly's official site includes a history of the game, news, tips and tricks, merchandise available for purchase, and the .com edition.

Nintendo
http://www.nintendo.com/
> Nintendo offers links to product sites like Gameboy and Pokémon as well as downloads, news, and merchandise.

Ringling Bros. and Barnum & Bailey
http://www.ringling.com/
　　This "online edition of The Greatest Show on Earth" features current show dates, a history of the circus, news, souvenirs, and fun and games.

Scrabble
http://www.scrabble.com/
　　This is the official World Wide Web site of the Scrabble game. It offers a history of the game, clubs and organizations, and information about the many levels of the game.

Magazine Web Sites
Designed Especially for Students

Consumer Reports Online for Kids
http://www.zillions.org/
　　This site, for kids eight years and older, replaces the print version of *Zillions* and offers consumer information on products and services.

Kids' Castle
http://www.kidscastle.si.edu/
　　Smithsonian magazine presents this exceptional site filled with a variety of information for students ages 8–16. Viewers can click on characters like Eddie (after Thomas Edison) or Aron (after Elvis Aron Presley) to learn about science, animals, personalities, and much more. In each area, there are articles with links to other sites based on the same subject.

Kids @ National Geographic
http://www.nationalgeographic.com/kids
　　This site from *National Geographic* is well organized and offers quality information in a kid-friendly format. Users can create cartoons, play interactive games, learn jokes and riddles, try science experiments, correspond with a pen pal, and even participate in a family interactive activity.

Odyssey
http://www.odysseymagazine.com/
　　This "web site of the award-winning science magazine for young readers, ages 10–16," offers resources for students and teachers. The site offers links to live Web cams, science articles, teacher resources, information about the current issue of the magazine, and much more.

Sports Illustrated for Kids
http://www.sikids.com/
　　From basketball to football, hockey to racing, this site offers almost everything for the student interested in sports. Users can play cool interactive games, participate in fantasy sports leagues, take trivia challenges, seek sports advice, and more. The site also offers an online version of the current issue of the magazine.

Newspapers and Magazines

The following Web sites are just a sampling of the extensive newspapers and magazines that can be found by accessing their Web sites. Many of the periodicals are available online. The sites offer information on current events, entertainment, fashion, sports, and much more. To find such sites for other newspapers and magazines, any general search engine (Yahoo, Lycos) offers a listing organized by subject.

National Geographic
   http://www.nationalgeographic.com/

Newsweek
   http://school.newsweek.com/

Sports Illustrated
   http://sportsillustrated.cnn.com/

Time
   http://www.time.com/

U.S. News and World Report
   http://www.usnews.com/

Sports

Baseball, football, skating, soccer . . . although the Web offers sites for almost every imaginable sport, the safest sites for students are the official sites of the sport. These official sites have up-to-date information about activities, players, statistics, history, and much more. Many sites even offer online shopping for official memorabilia. An added feature of some of the sites is links to local teams or organizations that support that particular sport.

*Kids World 2000 Sports Around the World
   http://now2000.com/kids/sports.shtml
      Kids World 2000 also offers links to "Sports Around the World" including martial arts, ping-pong, tennis, track and field, and many others, as well as links to Olympic sites.

Major League Baseball
   http://www.majorleaguebaseball.com/
      Baseball news, special features, statistics, standings, schedules, and information about players can be found at this popular site. While here, visitors may want to listen to a live game on audio or view one daily on video.

NASCAR
   http://www.nascar.com/
      This site provides news, race results, schedules, standings, and team information about NASCAR. A store is also available to visitors.

National Basketball Association
http://www.nba.com/

News releases, special features, statistics, team schedules, and the NBA store are available online. Students will also enjoy viewing information about the players and the history of basketball.

National Football League
http://www.nfl.com/

This popular site contains news, statistics, and team standings as well as information about the players. The special area designed for kids offers football facts, games, and interesting activities. The "QB Club" and "Coaches Club" allow visitors to chat online with quarterbacks and coaches.

U.S. Figure Skating
http://www.usfsa.org/

Visit this site for news and information about figure-skating events, the athletes, and contest results. Links make up the bulk of this site. "Clubs" lists USFSA clubs around the United States and "Synch" focuses on synchronized team skating.

U.S. Soccer
http://www.us-soccer.com/

This official Web site of the U.S. Soccer Federation contains sections on media, publications, national teams, members, coaching, and referees.

*Yahooligans
http://www.yahooligans.com/Sports_and_Recreation/

This address provides links to selected sites based on teen appeal.

RESOURCES TO SUPPORT MEDIA SPECIALISTS AND TEACHERS

Resources that support programming for professionals can be accessed at many of the Web sites throughout this chapter. Here, we specifically list sites that are either exceptional for various educational disciplines, or of particular interest to teachers in individual subject areas.

Copyright

Because school library media specialists are constantly asked about and often made responsible for copyright information, we have created a special section to offer support in that area. Although you probably have considerable knowledge about copyright in general, with every new medium comes another set of standards that we all must follow. We hope these sites answer some of your questions.

Copyright and Fair Use
http://fairuse.stanford.edu/

Stanford University Libraries developed this site devoted to information about copyright and fair use. The site is organized into the following categories: "Primary Materials"; "Current Legislation, Cases, and Issues"; "Resources on the Internet"; and "Overview of Copyright Law."

Copyright and Intellectual Property
http://www.ala.org/work/copyright.html

This ALA site offers a link to the Association of College and Research Libraries where users can find information and links on copyright protection, fair use, and intellectual property.

Copyright Crash Course
http://www.utsystem.edu/OGC/IntellectualProperty/cprtindx.htm

Although the University of Texas Administration Office of General Counsel developed this crash course in copyright information for its faculty, other users can benefit from the information. The section that discusses fair use is well organized, easy to understand, and offers "tests" to check for adherence to fair use.

Copyright: Frequently Asked Questions
http://web.mit.edu/cwis/copyright/faq.html

The MIT Copyright Working Group developed this site that answers 16 frequently asked questions about copyright, including "What is fair use?" and "Can I copy films and videos?" The answers are straightforward and easy to understand.

The Copyright Web Site
http://www.benedict.com/

Besides looking at copyright issues as applied to visual, audio, and digital arts, this site offers a section called "The Basics," which outlines information on fair use, public domain, copyright registration and forms, and copyright protection.

U.S. Copyright Office
http://lcweb.loc.gov/copyright/

General information, publications, legislation, records, announcements, and links are found at this site, an area of the Library of Congress. Users can learn copyright basics and registration procedures as well as find all necessary forms.

Curriculum

ArtsEdge
http://artsedge.kennedy-center.org/

The John F. Kennedy Center for the Performing Arts and the National Endowment for the Arts established this site to help "educators to teach in, through, and about the arts." The site is organized into "NewsBreak," "Teaching Materials," and "Professional Resources." Under "Teaching Materials," users can find lessons, activities, and links, as well as a publishing area and idea exchange. The lessons and activities can be viewed either by subjects such as foreign language, science, and the arts, or viewed by grade levels. The lesson plans are well organized and easy to implement.

Edsitement
http://edsitement.neh.gov/

The National Endowment for the Humanities developed this "best of the humanities on the web" and includes the subject areas of literature and language arts, foreign language, art and culture, and history and social studies. Each area is organized by grade level. The site also includes Web sites, lesson plans, references, and teachers' resources.

Photo 6.2. The health teacher guides students through an Internet search for the "What's Up Doc: Discovering Diseases" program that he and the library media specialist developed together. *(Russell Middle School, Omaha, Nebraska, Millard Public Schools)*

Health Teacher
http://www.healthteacher.com/

The site "provides a comprehensive, sequential K–12 health education curriculum that consists of almost 300 lesson plans that meet National Health Education Standards and provide skills-based assessment methods." The lesson guides are organized first by subject (alcohol and other drugs, community and environmental health, injury prevention) and then by grade level.

K–12 Resources for Music Educators
http://www.isd77.k12.mn.us/resources/staffpages/shirk/k12.music.html

The site's resources are organized by band, orchestra, vocal, classroom music, and all music teachers. Most listed resources provide the link and a short description of the site. Other areas of this site include: "Music Research Resources"; "Biographies, History, and Works of Great Composers"; "MIDI Resources"; and "Music Newsgroups."

P.E. Central
http://pe.central.vt.edu/

This "ultimate web site for Health and Physical Education Teachers" offers a huge variety and quantity of information. Users can find information on assessments, books and music, research, instructional resources, and much more. The site includes a store, a job center, and schedules of upcoming workshops. The "lesson ideas" are organized in 13 categories including instant activities; health; preschool, K–2, 3–5, and middle/high school; lesson plans; field day ideas; and more.

General Resources

*Awesome Library
http://www.awesomelibrary.org/Library/Reference_and_Periodicals
/Librarian_Information/Librarian_Information.html

This site "organizes the Web with 14,000 carefully reviewed resources including the top five percent in education," and offers an area just for librarians. Under "Librarian Information," there are over 90 links to sites of interest to librarians. The sites are organized by discussions, lesson plans, lists, materials, papers, purchase resources, and recommendations. The resources presented include book resources, book reviews, citations, encyclopedia search, associations, clip art, Dewey Decimal information, libraries on the Web, OCLC, and much more. Some of the suggested sub-topics are acceptable use policies, library catalogs, citations, and public libraries.

Blue Web'n Learning Sites Library
http://www.kn.pacbell.com/wired/bluewebn/

This "library of Blue Ribbon learning sites on the Web" offers wonderful lesson plans for integrating the Internet into classroom learning. The site is updated weekly with new lessons described by subject area, grade level, and application type. The lessons are also rated with a star system.

*Eduhound
http://eduhound.com/

T.H.E. Journal sponsors this site of "Everything for Educators K–12." Users first choose a category from the extensive listing that includes administration, library and research, virtual explorations, and much more. The category then lists topics followed by the links. Each link includes a short description and the URL. For example, under "Library and Research-Librarian," there are 33 sites listed including links to associations, lesson plans, and resource sites.

*ERIC Links
http://ericir.syr.edu/

This ERIC site offers "Library and Information Science Links"; "Educational Technology Links"; "K–12 Education, Technology, and the Internet Links"; and other ERIC links. Recommended sites include: "ALA's Links to Library Web Resources," "Big 6 Information Problem Solving," "The Internet Public Library (IPL)," and "Library of Congress."

A Guide to Internet Resources (American Association for the Advancement of Science)
http://www.aaas.org/ehr/slic/internet.html

The American Association for the Advancement of Science (AAAS) developed this site as "a starting point for you for finding Internet Resources." This extensive listing compiled in May 2000 includes a variety of resources for subjects like math, general science, bioscience, health, college and financial aid, career study, software review, and many others. The sites "have been reviewed by scientific organizations; were created by schools, scientists, or other reputable organizations; and/or have won awards for quality." Some of the quality sites listed include the Eisenhower National Clearinghouse for Math and Science Education, The National Civil Rights Museum, and *National Geographic*.

ICONnect: KidsConnect
http://www.ala.org/ICONN/kidsconn.html

The goal of this site "is to help students access and use the information available on the Internet effectively and efficiently." Volunteer school librarians provide direct assistance to students via e-mail within two school days. The site also lists favorite Web sites by subject.

Information Searcher's CyberTours
http://www.infosearcher.com/cybertours

This site is an electronic extension of *Internet for Active Learners: K–12 Curriculum Strategies* by Pam Berger (ALA Editions, 1998) and guides users through CyberTours, "a series of 12 to 15 pre-selected Web sites focusing on a particular curriculum theme." The cybertour is organized by "Active Learning Sites," "Search Strategies," "Web Evaluation Guide," "Weaving a Web-Based Curriculum," "Reference on the Web," "Planning Your Library Web Site," and "Teaching the Internet."

Internet School Library Media Center
http://falcon.jmu.edu/~ramseyil/

Professor Inez Ramsey of James Madison University's Library Science Program developed this site with resources "of possible interest to librarians and teachers in the electronic library." Users will find sites for all subject areas, professional resources, reference sources, selection aids, technology, publishers, and much more.

*Kathy Schrock's Guide for Educators
http://discoveryschool.com/schrockguide/

Kathy Schrock, a former librarian who is now a technology coordinator, designed this site as "a categorized list of sites on the Internet found to be useful for enhancing curriculum and teacher professional growth." The site is organized according to numerous subject areas that may support library programs. Information for training educators on using the Internet can also be found at this information-packed resource.

*Library and Information Science Resources: A Library of Congress Internet Resource Page
http://lcweb.loc.gov/global/library/

The Library of Congress offers an extensive site filled with important links for librarians. Links are organized by "General Resources," "National Libraries (United States and Foreign)," "Library Home Pages," "School Library Resources," "Online Catalogs," "Research and Reference," "Technical Services," "Special Collections," "Professional Organizations," "Library and Information Science Schools," "Professional Journals," "Library Vendors," and "Library Conferences." The "Library Vendor" area uniquely offers links to some of the most popular vendors for the library.

*Library Spot Librarian's Shelf
http://www.libraryspot.com/librarian.htm

The Library Spot site offers a wide variety of resources about libraries and reference. For the school librarian, the best area is the "Librarian's Shelf" with links to the following: "Associations," "General Tools/Resources," "Libraries and the Internet," "Mailing Lists/Newsgroups," "Library Journals," and "Acquisitions, and Cataloging." In the "Libraries & the Internet" area, there are excellent links for library Web managers. The "Y.A. Services" area offers links to YALSA, The ALAN Review, and other young adult sites.

*LION: An Information Resource for K–12 School Librarians
http://www.libertynet.org/lion/lion.html

As one of the best sites for school librarians, the Librarians Information Online Network (LION) offers extensive information and links on subjects such as library automation, cataloging resources, CD-ROMs, lesson plans, forums, and organizations. The area, "Issues in School Librarianship," offers especially useful links and resources about issues affecting school librarians today including copyright and fair use, programming, scheduling, facilities, and staffing. The site is sponsored by Library Services of the School District of Philadelphia.

*LM_NET on the Web
http://ericir.syr.edu/lm_net/

"LM_NET is a discussion group open to school library media specialists worldwide, and to people involved with the school library media field." Librarians use this discussion-group site to ask for information, share ideas, link programs, and network. Users can subscribe to the group and immediately begin to view or use the site.

School Library Resources on the Internet
http://www.iasl-slo.org/

The International Association of School Librarianship (IASL) created this site to "take teacher librarians to the best 'starting points' for Internet exploration." The resource list includes library and school library associations, school library Web sites, resources for school librarians, information skills resources, automation resources, and reading promotion resources. The site is "necessarily selective" and discusses the selection criteria. The site also offers "Creating a Web Page for Your School Library."

*700+ Great Sites: Amazing, Spectacular, Mysterious, Colorful Web Sites for Kids and the Adults Who Care About Them
http://www.ala.org/parentspage/greatsites/

This list of sites compiled by the Children and Technology Committee of the Association for Library Services to Children, a division of the ALA, offers links to "Library/School Sites"; "Sites for Children"; and "Sites for Parents, Caregivers, Teachers, and Others Who Care About Kids," where librarians can find links to associations and online journals.

Yahooligans! Teachers' Guide
http://www.yahooligans.com/tg/

This area of the search engine *Yahooligans* provides wonderful information and lessons for educators. Sample lesson plans are offered "for planning, implementing, and assessing integrated Internet units." Lessons focus on a variety of subjects such as bats, birds, Earth Day, and the Constitution. The plans are well organized and easy to implement.

Professional Associations

*AASL: American Association of School Librarians
http://www.ala.org/aasl/

National standards and guidelines, professional and Internet resources, news about hot topics, and a list of related organizations with links can be found at this site. Also available is a helpful directory with links to state library Web sites, the Library of Congress, and state and regional affiliated organizations of library media specialists.

AECT: Association for Educational Communications and Technology
http://www.aect.org/

"The mission of the Association for Educational Communications and Technology is to provide leadership in educational communications and technology by linking professionals holding a common interest in the use of educational technology and its application to the learning process." The site offers a link to the association's online journal, *Educational Technology Research & Development*.

ALAN: The Assembly on Literature for Adolescents of the National Council of the Teachers of English
http://engfac.byu.edu/resources/alan/

This special interest group of The National Council of the Teachers of English developed this site for those "who are particularly interested in the area of young adult literature." This site provides the online version of the association's journal, *The ALAN Review*, as well as information about the ALAN Award for "an outstanding individual in the field of adolescent literature." The site also offers links to other young adult literature resources.

*Education Week
http://www.edweek.org/context/orgs/subject_orgs.htm

This site lists all the major organizations and associations involved in education and arranges them by topics such as administration, health and safety, mathematics, parent involvement, and teacher organizations. The listing offers more background information and links to the association or organization's site.

International Reading Association (IRA)
http://www.reading.org/

"The International Reading Association seeks to promote high levels of literacy for all by improving the quality of reading instruction through studying the reading process and teaching techniques; serving as a clearinghouse for the dissemination of reading research through conferences, journals, and other publications; and actively encouraging the lifetime reading habit." The association's site offers association and membership information, news and research articles, conference and projects information, literacy links, and publications. The "Choices Booklists" area offers the "Young Adults' Choices" for each year as published in the *Journal of Adolescent and Adult Literacy*, an IRA publication.

NASSP: National Association of Secondary School Principals
http://www.nassp.org/

This national organization serves educational leaders in middle and high schools. Goals for the organization, membership information, a calendar of events, and hot topics and issues in education can be found at this site.

NCTE Middle
http://www.ncte.org/middle/

Besides the *ALAN* site, the National Council of Teachers of English offers its own site with a link to resources dedicated to the "middle" grades. The most useful resource is the MiddleWeb Index, a "topical index that will take you directly to some of the most useful documents and links on the MiddleWeb site" (links dedicated to research and information about the middle-school student). The site also includes "Tech Connect Links" from the *Voices in the Middle* journal with links to "electronic forms of storytelling and online resources by some experts on language arts classroom practice."

NCTM: National Council of Teachers of Mathematics
http://www.nctm.org/

The National Council of Teachers of Mathematics, "dedicated to the highest-quality mathematics education for all students," developed this site to support mathematics education. Users can find the typical association information (membership, conferences/events, publications/products) and "News & Hot Topics." The "Teachers' Corner" offers "Professional Development Opportunities," "Web Resources," and "Teaching Resources and Activities for Your Classroom."

NSTA: National Science Teachers Association
http://www.nsta.org/

"Promoting excellence and innovation in science teaching and learning for all," this NSTA site offers a great "Online Resources" area. Here, users can find all of the NSTA journals online, science suppliers and programs, National Science Education Standards, an extensive listing of recommended Web sites, and other professional resources. Under "NSTA Recommends," there are "popular reviews of the science-teaching materials that were previously only available in print." Reviewed titles can be searched by title/key word, author's name, grade, category, and subject. The reviews give the material's bibliographic information and a two- or three-paragraph review.

SocialStudies.org
http://www.ncss.org/

This site developed by the National Council for Social Studies helps to support the association's mission "to provide leadership, service, and support for all social studies educators." As with the other association sites, information is provided about the association, its membership, news, legislation, position statements, and state and local councils. The site offers a "Teaching Resources" area "categorized by the ten themes of the Curriculum Standards for Social Studies." The "Notable Social Studies Trade Books for Young People" are listed in an easy to print bibliography format. Another area to note is the "Media Watch," which lists television and radio programs that support social studies themes.

Young Adult Library Services Association
http://www.ala.org/yalsa/

The site states, "The goal of the Young Adult Services Division is to advocate, promote and strengthen service to young adults as part of the continuum of total library service." This division of the ALA offers resources dedicated to the young adult reader. The site offers information about the association itself as well as membership, professional resources, young adult sites, state and local news, and conference and event schedules. There are also areas for "Awards & Special Projects" and "Winning Titles."

Professional Journals

Booklist
http://www.ala.org/booklist/

The Horn Book
http://www.hbook.com/

School Library Journal Online
http://slj.reviewsnews.com/

Teacher Librarian: The Journal for School Library Professionals
http://www.teacherlibrarian.com/

Special Middle School Sites

Caught in the Middle
http://www.caughtinthemiddle.org/

  This "web guide for parents of middle school students," funded in part by the U.S. Department of Education, offers a "28 minute video project and comprehensive web site that encourages parents to stay involved in their children's lives during the often-tumultuous middle school years." The resources page offers a listing of online resources, books, journals, periodicals, newsletters, and organizations.

Eastchester Middle School Terrific Web Sites Just for Middle School Kids
http://www.westnet.com/~rickd/Kids.html

  This listing of sites for the middle-school audience includes visual and performing arts; computer and technology; English; health; mathematics; science; social studies; sports; town, country, and state; and fun and entertainment. The recommended sites range from the Louvre to computer manufacturers to the San Diego Zoo and more.

Middle Level Leadership Center
http://www.mllc.org/

  Established in the Department of Educational Leadership and Policy Analysis at the University of Missouri "to promote quality middle level education through the development and dissemination of knowledge about effective site-level leadership," this site offers research, surveys, and presentations. The site's extensive list of Web links is organized by "Journals," "Organizations and Centers," "Researching/Finding Information," "Teaching and Learning," and "Miscellaneous."

MiddleWeb
http://www.middleweb.com/

  This "World Wide Web site exploring the challenges of middle school reform and brimming with resources for educators and parents" offers updates, news, links, and a "topical index that will take you directly to some of the most useful documents and links on the *MiddleWeb* site." These topics include "Assessment and Evaluation," "Curriculum and Instruction," "Parents and the Public," "Student and School Life," and "Teachers at Work." At each topic, you will find documents and approved Web sites.

National Middle School Association
http://www.nmsa.org/

  This site, "devoted to improving the educational experiences of young adolescents," shares information about the organization, news, an online bookstore, professional development opportunities, services and resources, and a members-only area. Under "Services/Resources," there is a listing of useful Web sites.

CONCLUSION

The Internet offers such a wealth of information that it has become almost impossible to imagine developing a program without using it to find resources, or accessing it to enhance program ideas. Whether you are skilled enough to develop your own database that bookmarks worthwhile sites similar to those listed in this chapter or are simply embarking on Web tours for the first time, the Internet is an astounding, and ever-more invaluable tool for programming.

Extending, Evaluating, and Assessing Library Media Programs

No matter how successful the event, all good programs need to be followed up. Media specialists often create written activities that solidify or extend learning. An equally effective alternative is to construct a special display or teach an extension lesson before school, after school, or during lunch.

Also, your work is not complete until you have thanked everyone who helped plan and present the program. Whether formally or informally, be sure to thank guest speakers, volunteers, and colleagues who contributed materials or ideas.

Finally, you should also conduct formal evaluations to assess your program's merits and weaknesses. Although any tasks carried out after the major event itself may seem anticlimactic, they are relevant and necessary for teaching students, for acknowledging guests and volunteers, and for enabling you to improve subsequent programs.

EXTENDING THE PROGRAM

As you've intended, students' primary learning will occur during the program itself. Yet even if your presentation meaningfully covered every objective, student learning should be solidified through follow-up activities. Your continuation may extend learning or reinforce the information shared; ideally, it will do both while also inviting students to explore a topic more thoroughly on their own.

Activities for Students in the School Library Media Center

Our book fair lasts for two days after the Winter Wonderland event. During the extended time, students can continue visiting the library media center to make final purchases. Interestingly, we actually see an increase in sales during those days. I think that parents sometimes look over the items during the Winter Wonderland with their children and then allow them to actually make the purchases on their own.

While planning your program, consider some good follow-up activities to share after the event. Depending on their complexity, these activities may demand various amounts of time to complete. For example, one multicultural program featured a display titled "Global Wardrobe" that included sketches of various ethnic dress. In the follow-up activity for this display, the media specialist invited the geography/social studies teacher to explain why certain types of dress developed because of regional climate (parkas versus saris, for example) and because of cultural beliefs (piercings, veils).

Instead of follow-up lessons, some media specialists use interest centers as a means of extending a program. Instead of the "Worldwide Wardrobe" extension lesson, the library media specialist could have created an interest center with articles of clothing from various cultures, maps indicating climate differences, photographs of people from different groups wearing unique garb, and reading material and questions that allowed for independent learning.

Following a program, book displays and bulletin boards make great extended activities in your library media center. Promoting books on your program topic effectively extends learning, and the circulation of these titles often increases. Ideally, books placed on display are checked out immediately.

Activities for Students in the Classroom

We follow up the Winter Wonderland event with many activities for students in the classroom. Rather than do just one, we often have students choose from a variety of creative learning assignments that include:

- Complete word searches and play games about holiday music that teachers use with students in the classroom during the last few days before the holiday break.

- Read aloud Charles Dickens' A Christmas Carol.

- Create holiday cards for local nursing homes and day care centers.

- Learn holiday poetry and recite it for other teachers and classes, staff, and administrators.

- Do a mini research project on various winter holidays including Christmas, Hanukkah, Kwanzaa, and Chinese New Year.

- After hearing the principal or other staff member read portions of A Cowboy Night Before Christmas by James Rice over the morning broadcast announcements, they write and illustrate their own versions of this exciting story.

- Work in groups to create multimedia presentations with video, pictures, and text of various winter holidays around the world.

- Create a memory box. They can decorate the box with lively holiday ornamentation and then invite friends, teachers, and family members to write down their favorite holiday memory to place in the box. They can then share some of these memories with the class.

Some of the best follow-up activities can be generated by teachers and offered in the classroom. To support their efforts, provide them with a bibliography of trade books, reference resources, and Web site addresses related to the subject. If you have a district professional library, order related materials and inform teachers that you have them on reserve for their use.

If you feel comfortable doing so, you can even carry your support a step further by recommending classroom activities. Remember, although teachers are experts in their general subject area, your deep and extensive programming work makes you the most informed and up-to-date aficionado of that particular program topic. Consequently, many teachers will gladly use your follow-up activities, and most will appreciate your doing the work to create them.

Like extension work that you offer in the media center, follow-up activities for the classroom may include program-related learning centers, games, worksheets, art, and writing assignments. If you create the follow-up activity, keep copies of it in your program file. If teachers develop classroom activities that extend your program, ask for a copy of their work and file it with your program materials as well.

COMPLETING THE PROCESS

Follow-up activities fulfill the last teaching component of your program. But you still have two significant details to cover before your work is done. The first involves extending a simple courtesy that tremendously impacts your program participants. The second gives your program closure and enables you to determine how successfully your learning objectives were met.

Thank Your Resource People

The power of gratitude resonates loud and long. More than any other interaction with program participants and volunteers, acknowledging their work and efforts creates a positive ripple effect that benefits them, you, and the entire school. Immediately following the special event, express your appreciation to the resource people and/or companies that participated in the program.

No matter how simple or elaborate your program, acknowledge the speaker or business. You may thank them in several ways. For some guests, sending a handwritten thank-you note is appropriate. To speakers representing a company or business, send a formal thank-you, typed on letterhead stationery. Also ask speakers if they would like you to send a letter to the business they represented. It would seem appropriate to do so in all situations. However, library media specialists have occasionally found themselves in an uncomfortable situation. After sending a letter to the business, they discovered that the speaker had not secured permission to participate in the program on company time. Although such instances are rare, they are worth noting so that all acknowledgments fulfill their positive intent.

In many cases, principals are willing to send thank-you letters to program speakers on behalf of the program participants, or even the students or school in general. A letter from the principal written on school letterhead adds a professional touch that enhances the school's image. Even if your principal agrees to send formal acknowledgments, you should still send thank-you notes to those participants, too.

Rather than sending notes, you may prefer to present certificates or plaques of appreciation to your participants. You may do so individually, or, for a more public acknowledgment, you might recognize presenters and volunteer staff at a luncheon, breakfast, or similar event. No matter how you express your thanks, your thoughtfulness will be remembered for a long time and will make volunteers more receptive to future requests for program assistance.

Some of the best thank-yous come from students. Encourage them to develop a life-long habit of writing thank-you notes. Formal expressions of gratitude are always appropriate, and always meaningful, for both the person who gives thanks and the one who receives it. As an alternative, you might encourage students to videotape or audiotape their thank-yous. If you have the equipment in your school library media center, you might even model the behavior, or work with them to ensure a quality presentation. Whatever manner seems most appropriate, express gratitude to your resource people.

Thank Your Volunteers

Over the years, I have thanked my volunteers in many ways. For students, I have made cards, given candy, and created special ornaments. For the staff, I provide a breakfast in appreciation for their help. I also use the school's broadcast announcements to publicly thank everyone involved in the program. This year, I plan to give a special bookmark to the student participants and am considering hosting a special snacks and wassail party for the staff following Winter Wonderland.

Acknowledge all your volunteer help with a handwritten note, typed letter, or certificate of appreciation. Send thank-you notes to teachers, volunteers, parents, ancillary staff, the PTA, and any other people who supported the program. Even if you show your appreciation to all your volunteers with a special year-end reception, you should still express gratitude in some form immediately following your program.

Update the Community Resources File

Even though volunteers will be updating your community resources file at least once a year, you should also update it after your program. Add new information and eliminate any that is outdated. To update your files:

- Record a brief explanation of how you used the resources for the program.

- Correct, add, or delete information such as fees, contact persons, and supplemental resources.

- Include information on any new features incorporated into the program.

- Write a brief summary of positive and negative responses from students and teachers.

- Add new resources to the file.

- Delete files if necessary.

Part of the update should include making notations about the community resource people. Beyond their general effectiveness as presenters, note whether their ideas and vocabulary were appropriate to students. Recall your observations during the presentation. Did the speaker establish and maintain a positive rapport with the audience? Was there an appropriate blend of sharing useful information and connecting meaningfully with the students? That synergy alone is worth noting, and worth remembering when securing speakers for future programs.

Assessing the topic is equally important. Ask yourself such questions as: Did it pique students' interest as much as I had hoped? Was the material appropriate to my audience? Did it provide relevant and dynamic curriculum support? Record your answers in the community resources file and review them before presenting the program again.

EVALUATING THE PROGRAM

To determine your program's success, you have access to several effective evaluation options. Some involve informal observations that you can make during program presentations. Others include formal tools that provide concrete feedback for assessing several elements of your program. By using both types of evaluation, you can clearly identify your program strengths.

Thus far, I have used no formal evaluation form to assess the program. I do, however, talk over the success and some challenges of the program with the library aide, administrative team, fine arts department, and other teachers. In general, we feel that this is a successful program that does accomplish all the objectives that we set forth in the beginning. From our observations, the staff and I agree that parents really enjoy this evening each year.

Every year we change the program slightly to better serve our audience and focus the evening on the book fair and our student performers. For example, from one brainstorming evaluation session, we determined that our method of letting guests get their own refreshments was both inequitable and too time-consuming. We tossed around some ideas until we came up with a much better plan for this coming year. Instead of having elaborate tables where participants help themselves to refreshments, we will set up two large tables. At the table in the middle of the room, parent volunteers will serve punch. On a large table in the corner of the room we will place colorful baskets inside of which will be Ziploc® baggies filled with holiday cookies. Students and teachers will give one bag to each individual.

How will we keep up with whether or not the person has been given a treat? When the visitors come to the school, they are going to be asked to donate a canned good. We will then issue them a ticket that they can exchange for cookies. We hope this solves some of our problems with people getting more than their share.

We also discussed the success and challenges of the program in general faculty meetings. During one of those sessions, teachers shared some great ideas about extending the program. One teacher suggested we secure more community involvement by inviting a local church to bring their handbell choir to join in the performance. Another teacher recommended we ask either a school board member or local personality to join the program by reading some poetry or perhaps singing.

I discovered that including teachers and administrators in these informal assessments adds greatly to their sense of ownership in the program, which in turn leads to more enthusiasm and commitment by them and their students.

Informal Evaluations

Most educators instinctively make informal evaluations. Both blatant and subtle nonverbal reactions by students during programs can indicate weak points in content or presentation. Written feedback from participants also helps you determine how much the program met your learning objectives.

By Library Media Specialist

Before formally evaluating the program, sit down after the event and reflect on how well you think it went. Did it meet your original goals? How did the audience react? Did the program hold their interest? What were the program's strengths? What went better than expected? What didn't have the impact you thought it would? Given the opportunity, what would you do differently? Trust your instincts. Even before asking, you often know how the program went.

By Faculty and Students

Next, consider essential feedback from faculty members and students. Their nonverbal cues during the presentation say much. Looks of interest or boredom on their faces during the program are as revealing as their comments. Opinions expressed during conversations, whether enthusiastic or critical, provide more clues for analyzing the success of the completed program and for developing future programs. Some media specialists jot down their observations; others record comments more thoroughly in a journal. Writing your perceptions and others' observations when they are still fresh can help tremendously as you embark on your next program.

An obvious programming goal is to motivate students to check out and read books in your collection. Therefore, observing students' and faculty members' subsequent visits to the media center can offer some insight. When students and teachers are really excited about a topic, related books circulate and media center use often increases, at least temporarily. Notice also if books on subjects even indirectly connected to your program topic begin circulating more. Finally, patrons' interest in browsing book displays and participating in interest center activities associated with the program also indicate a successful program.

Teachers' involvement in extended activities following the program reflects a successful program as well. Not surprisingly, **enthusiastic** responses to a strong program translate into long-term interest in the topic well **after the** event has ended. If a teacher extends student learning about your program topic by generating classroom lessons or activities without your request, then you know your work inspired them.

You can learn much by observing changes in teachers and students following the program. Aspire to find schoolwide enthusiasm for the topic. Seeing teachers use your program as a springboard for their classroom activities is a sure sign of program success. Noticing improved attitudes about the library media center by formerly disinterested students is another. Naturally, seeing students excited about the topic or skill related to the library program, responding to requests for more books on the topic, and helping students find more related resources in the reference section are all strong indicators of the program's impact.

Formal Evaluations

You can determine your program's strengths and weaknesses even more concretely through formal evaluations. By using some of the evaluation techniques and forms provided, you will get a very clear picture of exactly what participants experienced, felt, and even learned.

By Library Media Specialist

Immediately following the program, use the instrument in Figure 7.1 (which is based on the original program planning checklist) to evaluate its success. With this form, you can determine how the facility and support resources, as well as individual speakers, contributed to the overall effectiveness of your program. After you fill out this formal evaluation, analyze the data.

MEDIA SPECIALIST PROGRAM EVALUATION

Using the five-point Likert scale below, please circle the appropriate response that best describes how effectively the program item was met.

Program topic _____

Date of program _____ Location _____

PROGRAM CHECKLIST	INEFFECTIVE				EFFECTIVE
Interest for theme	1	2	3	4	5
Accomplished goals	1	2	3	4	5
Resources selected	1	2	3	4	5
Materials selected	1	2	3	4	5
Publicity	1	2	3	4	5
Scheduling process	1	2	3	4	5
Volunteers	1	2	3	4	5
Furniture and room arrangement	1	2	3	4	5
Seating arrangement	1	2	3	4	5
Traffic flow	1	2	3	4	5
Preparation of AV equipment	1	2	3	4	5
Lighting	1	2	3	4	5
Decorations, displays, exhibits	1	2	3	4	5
Guest speaker	1	2	3	4	5
OVERALL PROGRAM	**1**	**2**	**3**	**4**	**5**

Figure 7.1. Media specialist program evaluation form.

By Teachers

Formal evaluations by teachers and students are invaluable assessment tools. While the program is still fresh in their memories, ask them to complete simple forms listing clearly stated questions about the program. When developing the evaluation form, consider the following points:

- Seek feedback immediately following the program.

- Design a straightforward instrument that is easy to complete.

- Design an instrument that is easy to tabulate.

- Structure your questions carefully so as to obtain true reactions from respondents.

- Provide for open-ended comments.

- Assure anonymity for anyone completing the form.

- Collect the responses in a timely manner.

It is important to determine if teachers think that the program related to the curriculum and to students' needs. That feedback alone can determine whether you should offer a similar program in the future. Teacher responses also suggest other program needs. The faculty program response form in Figure 7.2 will help you.

OPINION NEEDED

Faculty Program Evaluation

Program topic _____

Date of program _____ Location _____

   Using the five-point Likert scale below, please circle your response to each statement that best describes the effectiveness of the school library media program.

	INEFFECTIVE				**EFFECTIVE**
ITEM					
Program topic met student interests	1	2	3	4	5
Program enriched the curriculum	1	2	3	4	5
Program provided new information	1	2	3	4	5
Speaker spoke at the right level	1	2	3	4	5
Speaker held audience's attention	1	2	3	4	5
OVERALL PROGRAM	**1**	**2**	**3**	**4**	**5**

Would you recommend that we invite this speaker back next year? Why or why not?
_____
_____

What other topics would you suggest for a school library media program?
_____
_____

List the strengths of the program.
_____
_____

Describe the weaknesses of the program.
_____
_____

Figure 7.2. Faculty program evaluation form.

By Students

To get the most genuine responses from students, have them fill out an evaluation form (see Figure 7.3) as soon after the program as possible. You can also design your own form.

WANTED!
YOUR OPINION ABOUT THE GUEST SPEAKER

Program topic _____

I enjoyed the speaker's presentation.	Yes _____ No _____
I learned new and useful information about the topic from this program.	Yes _____ No _____
I could hear the speaker well.	Yes _____ No _____
I could easily see the speaker and the material showed.	Yes _____ No _____
I want to find out more information about this topic.	Yes _____ No _____
I read at least one book on the topic before the program.	Yes _____ No _____
I want to read a book about the topic soon.	Yes _____ No _____
I would like to attend another special program in the school library media center.	Yes _____ No _____
I thought the program was too long.	Yes _____ No _____
I thought the program was too short.	Yes _____ No _____

The **best** aspect of the program was:

_____

_____

The **least** appealing or effective part of the program was:

_____

_____

I would like the school library media center to sponsor a program about (consider major subject areas, electives, and even personal interests):

_____

_____

PLEASE RETURN THIS FORM TO THE SUGGESTION BOX
IN THE SCHOOL LIBRARY MEDIA CENTER.

Figure 7.3. Sample program evaluation for students.

Circulation Data and Usage

As stated earlier, the two major goals of every program are to increase book circulation and school library media center usage. Following your program, examine circulation records. Do you see a marked increase in books and materials checked out on the program topic? Who is checking out the materials: teachers, students, or both? The data should provide you with the number of books circulated, types of books circulated, and the populations who checked them out. A significant increase in circulation immediately following a program usually confirms its success.

Examining the number of classes (and grade levels) that visit your media center also gives some indication of program success. Circulation data is also an important program evaluation tool and will shed light on whether future programs on the topic have the potential to garner enthusiastic responses.

ASSESSING THE PROGRAM

After gathering data from students, teachers, and your own records, you can complete your assessment. Sometimes, the feedback will align very closely with your own assessment of the program's success. Other times, you will gain new insights worth having. Best of all, formal data from several respondents enables you to find consistent patterns that strengthen the value of the feedback. For example, if only a handful of students claim that the guest speaker spoke too fast or was confusing, their opinion may be more about them than the speaker. But if that feedback appears consistently from many respondents, then it is worth considering.

Examine and Analyze the Data

Once you've collected and recorded the data, examine and analyze it. Note, however, that all data are not quantifiable. You must also take into consideration qualitative data. Look at the reported strengths and weaknesses of the program gleaned from the comments. With this data, you should be able to answer two questions: (1) Should I offer this program again? (2) If so, what can I do to make it better the next time?

Informal Data

Informal data consists of both general and specific comments, enthusiastic or disgruntled responses, and observable shifts in library media center patronage following the event. Although these data are not as measurable as statistical feedback, it is worth using to sharpen your overview of the program's effectiveness.

Formal Data

Evaluation Forms Data. As soon as students and teachers return their completed evaluations, analyze the data and then use the results to plan future programs. Their input should provide a clear picture of the program's strengths and weaknesses. It should also reinforce once and for all your conclusion about whether or not you met your goals. Even if your program was a resounding success, you should still compile a list of ways to improve, strengthen, or possibly modify future programs on the same topic. If nothing else, adding just a little variety will keep the program fresh and inviting to you. Also, among the data you may find several suggestions for other program topics worth presenting to students or teachers.

In addition to feedback on program content, the evaluations will also help you assess logistical matters such as traffic flow, seating, and other elements that usually must be determined by trial and error. Finally, use all feedback as an invitation to sharpen your skills and spur further creativity. Never take any suggestions personally. The feedback is not a reflection of you. It is only a tool to determine what you think worked well, what you believe is worth doing again, and what you would like to do differently the next time.

Circulation Data. Most programs include a goal to increase book circulation. In fact, media specialists occasionally develop programs that focus on a low-circulating area in the collection merely to get the books checked out. Following all programs, examine data for the next several months. Compare circulation for the months before and after the program. Note whether students and faculty members are checking out the books in the program category or related categories more frequently. Consider the number of materials circulated, the type of user (faculty, student, grade level, subject area), and types of materials (books, magazines, media). Considering all possible angles gives you a clear and accurate picture of your program's impact.

Record Data Results

When you have the results, you can immediately put them to good use. Determine whether you'll invite the speaker back and record your decision on that person's community resources card. If you'll be asking the speaker to return, record your own comments about him or her, as well as any relevant feedback from teachers and students. Also include notes about the program in general. The valuable information you've collected through assessment forms, personal notes, and statistical data will enable you to make thorough yet direct comments about the program for future reference. Kept in a well-organized resources file, the data and assessments will move you smoothly and swiftly through the planning stages of repeated or refined programs.

Develop a Program Report

Pull together the formal and informal data collected during and after the program. Write a report that specifies both the high points and the flaws of your program. Besides being a dynamic tool for you, the report is helpful to the school at large. Share all or portions of the report with your principal, who, if an effective administrator, will be interested in the data. Information gathered, such as increased circulation following the program (see Figure 7.4) and teachers' requests for specific book orders, will be vivid indicators of your facility's strengths and needs.

Your principal will probably include some of your data in reports to the district. Use this information to support budget requests for the library media center or to write grant proposals to fund your collection. As anyone who has written grant proposals knows, most grant requests are fulfilled because of need, not merely desire. What better way to demon-strate need than by including specific data accumulated before and after special programs?

Sharing this information with the principal also offers more personal benefits. Often, the self-assessment of your work will add markedly to your yearly evaluation, for your data is a concrete indicator that you have mastered the skill of creating effective programs and assessing their educational value.

PROGRAM DESCRIPTIVE STATISTICS

Program topic _____

Date of program _____ Location _____

Number of publicity notices appearing through local media _____

Number of classes invited to participate   _____

Number of classes actually participating   _____

Number of students participating in the program   _____

Number of volunteers   _____

Number of requests for additional information on topic   _____

Average weekly circulation of entire school prior to
program (for eight weeks)   _____

Average weekly circulation of entire school following
the program (for eight weeks)   _____

Miscellaneous notes:

_____

_____

_____

_____

Figure 7.4. Sample form for descriptive statistics.

Your report can include your original program plan, sample evaluation forms, results of the evaluations, comments by students and faculty members, and charts and graphs that dis-play the results. With all this information plainly laid out for the principal and school district administrators, they become more aware of all the demands and rewards of programming.

CONCLUSION

Although the excitement and anticipation of your work culminates on the actual day of the event, programs are never completed without the meaningful activities that bring closure to the entire process. To ensure that your learning objectives were met, offer follow-up activities in your school library media center. Or, extend learning to the classrooms by either sharing follow-up activities with teachers, or by suggesting possible lessons that recap the main content shared during your program. Even if you are unable to do anything more elaborate, compile and make available to teachers and students a bibliography or "For Further Exploration" list that students can use to research the topic in more detail if they want to.

Besides offering follow-up activities for students, find a meaningful way to acknowledge all those people and companies that made your program possible. Express your thanks in a timely manner. Even if you get the principal or students to help you, always find a personal way to express your gratitude.

Finally, gather and compile data about your program's effectiveness. Consistent data will give you a clear picture of the program's real value. Encapsulate those comments as succinctly as possible and keep them in a well-organized file for easy access in the future.

Clearly, the entire process of planning, presenting, and assessing programs blends creative freedom with logical steps that ensure solid results. From simple displays to elaborate events that include students, parents, and faculty members, programming is an excellent approach to sharing information. In the process, it can help you sustain your enthusiasm and generate interest in your school library media center from students, colleagues, administrators, and the community.

The impact of a program reaches far beyond your own school. Programs draw together members of the community. Parents interact with business representatives. Companies contributing resources add richly to the overall impact made on students. Volunteers from outside the school can view the faculty, school, and even education in a better light. Publicity generated by programs enhances the reputation of the school. Even groups who do not participate in the event hear about its impact from students, friends, and co-workers. With such far-reaching results, programming is certainly one of the most effective teaching strategies for reaching students, involving parents, including faculty members, and highlighting your library media center to your school, district, and community.

8

Dynamic Model Programs and Ideas

Even the most excited media specialists shared with us their concerns about finding the time and creative energy to develop programs. To address this issue, we selected 20 library media specialists from across the United States and gathered clear, well-developed program ideas that have already proved successful. The contributors are media specialists whose innovative approaches to teaching helped earn their exemplary middle schools the prestigious designation as a Blue Ribbon School by the U.S. Department of Education for 1999–2000.

Every contributing media specialist is known for exceptional programming. In addition to listing these outstanding professionals with their credentials at the beginning of this chapter, we include their names with each program idea they contributed. When no credit line appears, the program tip is a culmination of ideas submitted by three or more media specialists.

Some programs described in this chapter are entirely unique in content and presentation style. Others may have familiar contexts, but stand out in originality and community support in the form of speakers, volunteers, and resources.

This chapter highlights more than 70 model programs and ideas from across the United States. Some are original programs described in depth; others offer clever twists to familiar ideas. Feel free to use the program suggestions exactly as they appear or modify them to fit your particular needs. You may even want to design your own program by combining different ideas. In any case, let each contribution inspire you to develop your own programs.

The model programs and ideas are divided into three sections:

1. Programs for Students

2. Programs for Faculty

3. Programs for Community

CONTRIBUTORS OF MODEL SCHOOL LIBRARY PROGRAMS AND IDEAS

Sandy Bernahl
F.E. Peacock Middle School
1999–2000 Blue Ribbon School
Itasca School District #10
Itasca, Illinois
Outstanding Elementary Teachers of America
Teacher Learning Center in Des Plaines,
*   Illinois, Past President*
DuPage Library System Youth Advisory
Board, Board of Directors

Camille Burkard
Cresthill Middle School
1999–2000 Blue Ribbon School
Governor's Rating of Grade "A" School
Douglas County Schools
Parker, Colorado

Nancy Caplanis
Wolfe Middle School
1999–2000 Blue Ribbon School
Michigan Blue Ribbon School
Center Line Public Schools
Center Line, Michigan

Karen Toron Cooper
Montgomery Middle School
1999–2000 Blue Ribbon School
Montgomery Township Schools
Skillman, New Jersey
National Assessment for Educational
*   Progress (Technology Rich*
*   Environment Study)*

Diane O. Davis
Harry F. Byrd Middle School
1999–2000 Blue Ribbon School
Vanguard School
Henrico County Public Schools
Richmond, Virginia
Library Information Center Instructional
*   Idea Award*
Technology and Information Services
*   Action Plan, Henrico County Public*
*   Schools*
Volunteer at Whitehouse Conference of
*   Libraries and Information*

Lynne Hawkins
Sedgwick Middle School
1999–2000 Blue Ribbon School
West Hartford Public Schools
West Hartford, Connecticut
Connecticut Educational Media Association
*   Program Award*

Brian Joseph
Neptune Middle School
1999–2000 Blue Ribbon School
Florida Department of Education,
    Five Star Award
National Service Learning Leader School
Osceola County Schools
Kissimmee, Florida

Judy Koehl
Haggard Middle School
1999–2000 Blue Ribbon School
Plano Independent School District
Plano, Texas

Charleen (Char) Koppi
Rosemount Middle School
1999–2000 Blue Ribbon School
Independent School District 196
    (Rosemount, Apple Valley, Eagan)
Rosemount, Minnesota

Maureen Luebbers
Russell Middle School
1999–2000 Blue Ribbon School
Millard Public Schools
Omaha, Nebraska

Wayne Martin
Hand Middle School
1999–2000 Blue Ribbon School
Time magazine's Middle School of the Year
    for 2000, 2001
Governor's Award of Excellence
Palmetto's Finest
Richmond School District One
Columbia, South Carolina

Eileen Neill
Deer Creek Middle School
1999–2000 Blue Ribbon School
Jefferson County Public Schools
Littleton, Colorado

Nancy C. Owen
Harry F. Byrd Middle School
1999–2000 Blue Ribbon School
Henrico County Public Schools
Richmond, Virginia
Library Information Center Instructional
    Idea Award
Virginia Educational Media Association,
    Planning Committee
Virginia Educational Media Association,
    Archivist

Karen Paulus
First Colony Middle School
1999–2000 Blue Ribbon School
Texas Education Exemplary School
Fort Bend Independent School District
Sugar Land, Texas

Cindy Reinhart
South Oldham Middle School
1999–2000 Blue Ribbon School
Oldham County Schools
Crestwood, Kentucky

Noreen L. Shannon
Jackson Intermediate School
1999–2000 Blue Ribbon School
Pasadena Independent School District
Pasadena, Texas

Michele Soeder
Beachwood Middle School
1999–2000 Blue Ribbon School
Beachwood School District
Beachwood, Ohio
Award for Educational Excellence,
    Beachwood Schools

Marney Welmers
Tortolita Middle School
1999–2000 Blue Ribbon School
Marana Unified School District
Tucson, Arizona
National Science Foundation Fellow
National Council of Teachers of English
    "Promising Young Writers" State
    Coordinator

Miriam A. Wiese
Mesa Verde Middle School
1999–2000 Blue Ribbon School
California Distinguished School
Poway Unified School District
San Diego, California

Kathleen Yaeger
Neshaminy Middle School
2000–2001 Blue Ribbon School
Pennsylvania School of Distinction
Neshaminy School District
Langhorne, Pennsylvania

PROGRAMS FOR STUDENTS

Creating programs for students can be especially exciting because there are so many avenues open for program ideas. Beyond their varying educational needs and capabilities, students have diverse interests. So whether you're covering a topic from core curriculum or venturing out into topics that address students' personal interests, you should gain much insight from the following outstanding programs.

Curriculum:
English/Language Arts and Library

Author-Related Programs

❋ *Lynne Hawkins, Sedgwick Middle School, West Hartford Public Schools, West Hartford, Connecticut*

"Author-in-Residence"

The Author-in-Residence (AIR) program combines visits from a popular, prolific young adult author; a weekly trivia contest; and the incorporation of the author's works into classroom lesson plans. Originally developed by an English teacher and enthusiastically supported by the library media specialist, AIR's purpose is to get students to read more and to read for enjoyment and lifelong learning. Now a library-based program that involves 24 teachers and administrators, the entire school is reading, and program activities are constantly on the list of school events.

In June, Lynne and the teachers distribute summer reading lists. Students must read one book by the chosen author to fulfill part of the summer reading requirements. During September and October, teachers conduct booktalks about the author's books. Students read or listen to various titles by the author. By the time the author visits the school at the end of October, all 1,010 students are convinced that the author is a major celebrity, as indeed, she or he is.

Many additional exciting events go on at the school:

- Art students paint a mural based on the AIR's books.

- The media specialist hosts a weekly trivia contest.

- The Book Club, where students read and discuss a book by the AIR, meets weekly.

- "Battle of the Books." In January, teams are formed to begin preparation for the big March event: the "Battle of the Books," a Jeopardy/College Bowl-style contest based on the AIR's books that pits same-grade-level teams against one another. Using projectors and screens to show question values and scores, the contest almost outdoes the author visits in crowd excitement as each academic team cheers its team, biting its collective tongue to keep from blurting out answers. The "Battle of the Books" program developed by Electronic Bookshelf is library based. (Media specialists add their special twists to the original program.) A special committee (chaired by the media specialist) invests a lot of time into developing the questions and making the contest successful.

- Writer's workshop. The author returns in April, if it can be arranged, to hold a writer's workshop with students.

- Summer reading book fair. In June, the summer reading book fair and booktalks to incoming fifth graders kick off the next year's AIR program.

The program depends on the support of the entire staff and the participation of all students. The library media specialist, English teachers, administrators, a science teacher, the reading teachers, an art teacher, special education teachers, and a foreign-language teacher all contribute to running the program. Every student is involved, with accommodations for various learning styles.

The author visit is important, but it is also expensive. Well-known authors such as Norma Fox Mazer, Caroline Cooney, Will Hobbs, Avi, and poet Paul Janeczko have visited the school, and each was a real hit with the students. However, Lynne suggests that if you are unable to fund an author visit, the program can be centered on a popular author, without the visit. You can still use the various activities discussed here, and the program would still unify reading in the school. The books, however, are the single most important expense. Funding for Sedgwick Middle School is obtained through grants, book fairs, and from the PTO and a local civic organization.

The school, the students, the teachers, and the community reap the benefits from this exciting program. Because the entire school community is focusing on one author, Lynn finds students discussing the books among themselves and recommending favorite titles to one another. Comparisons are made to prior Authors-in-Residence; opinions are shared; literary conversations take place. Students choose books to read on their own. Diverse learning styles are accommodated by the widely varied activities. Audio books are available as needed, and teachers may choose to read aloud part or all of a book as a classroom reading activity.

School Library Journal (May 1993; April 2000) reported studies indicating that voluntarily reading self-selected books is the best way to improve both reading and writing skills. Media specialist Lynne Hawkins has certainly found this to be true. Reading self-selected books voluntarily is a part of Sedgwick's Author-in-Residence program, and from this program Lynne has seen impressive results. She emphasizes, "Students and teachers at Sedgwick Middle School are reading, and its book circulation, book fair sales, and community funding show it!"

✳ *Nancy Caplanis, Wolfe Middle School, Center Line Public Schools, Center Line, Michigan*

"Author Visits"

Students at Wolfe Middle School in Center Line, Michigan, enjoy visits by local authors and poets such as David Greenberg as well as by nationally recognized authors including Paula Danzinger. Following a dynamic and entertaining presentation, poet David Greenberg offered writing workshops for about 25 students from each grade. They brainstormed ideas and wrote about funny experiences they had encountered. He showed them how ideas are formed for poetry and novels. Proceeds from the media center book fairs fund these special author visits.

�֍ *Kathleen Yaeger, Neshaminy Middle School, Neshaminy School District, Langhorne, Pennsylvania*

"Tips for Preparing for an Author Visit"

- Review the available authors, their book titles, types of presentations, and fees.
- Discuss the candidates with team leaders and reading teachers.
- Select several dates that don't conflict with other activities or testing in your building.
- Contact the author to choose a date and communicate with the author on date, price, and program.
- Ask the author what equipment and other needs you can provide for the presentation day.
- Book the event up to a year in advance.
- Schedule the necessary rooms or auditorium.
- Order class sets of titles to be shared with students.
- Have extra copies of titles available for staff members to read.
- Use interlibrary loan when necessary.
- Allow enough time for reading the novels, discussion, and activities before the visit.
- Give each teacher a copy of background information on the author.
- Share ideas with teachers for publicizing the author.
- Involve the staff and students as much as possible.
- Include and involve special-area staff members as well.
- Allow students to research the background of the author and titles.
- Prepare and distribute order forms for students and staff to purchase a title by the author as a memento.
- Submit orders early enough so that they arrive ahead of the visit.
- Allow enough time before the visit to have the books autographed.
- Prepare a program for the special event.

Book Fairs

✳ *Camille Burkard, Cresthill Middle School, Douglas County Schools, Parker, Colorado*

"Book Fair at Cresthill"

As in most schools, the primary purpose of the Cresthill Book Fair is to raise money and awareness for the library program and to support literacy in the lives of the students. However, Camille adds several interesting twists to her book fair program by tapping community resources; enlisting the support of students, parents, and staff; and activating a communication blitz. The entire event serves to build a sense of community as all participants work together toward a common goal.

Camille began intensively planning the book fair in September. She interviewed two bookstore companies and compared the results of those interviews. She chose one well-known bookstore over the other because of the available dates and their genuine interest and willingness to work with her specific needs.

She selected November 30 because the timing coincided with holiday shopping for family and friends and allowed for a festive atmosphere so natural at that time of year. She began the event at 4:00 p.m. to allow enough time for set up after school and continued it until 8:30 p.m. so community members could drop in at their convenience and do some shopping while enjoying the music and social interactions.

After confirming the date with the school and the bookstore, she set general objectives using the following checklist.

1. Secure a staff of students and parents.

2. Offer student instruction sessions for poster making.

3. Teach gift-wrapping techniques.

4. Review greeting policies.

5. Generate publicity.

6. Gather supplies.

7. Cover details concerning book fair.

8. Secure entertainment.

9. Collaborate with teachers.

10. Order books.

Systematically, she addressed each area of preparation. To maintain an effective pace throughout the program development, she involved and supervised the three members of her library staff as well as student and parent volunteers.

Conducting a successful book fair for a large student body and community requires mobilizing many resources and coordinating a team of workers. More than 30 students worked on designing and contributing a variety of advertising posters and banners and setting up an elaborate display case for the book fair. They also attended training sessions where they learned or perfected their gift-wrapping techniques and practiced the etiquette of greeting customers at the bookstore. Eighteen parents were directly involved in preparing for and working at the actual event. In addition, 60 orchestra students, performing in various rotations, helped make this book fair a memorable success.

The entire event focused on reinforcing the importance of literacy as students and families connect with books at a local bookstore and join in supporting the school library program. The proceeds from the book fair made it possible to enlarge and update the library collection by purchasing quality reading and reference materials for the students, in both print and electronic formats. The book fair was a positive community-building event.

❋ *Karen Paulus, First Colony Middle School, Fort Bend Independent School District, Sugar Land, Texas*

"Book Fair at First Colony Middle School"

Many media specialists across the nation sponsor a book fair annually, but each year Karen Paulus sponsors two book fairs by two different local book fair companies. During these fairs, students preview and then purchase the books of their choice. Teachers also use this opportunity to provide titles for classroom reading, and Karen displays the titles from different teacher requests, along with the cost of the book.

The media center also sponsors special drawings and book giveaways. Students can register to win a book at the book fair (approximately 20 free books are given out). Since the first fair is in November, it often sparks ideas for holiday gift giving. Karen also sets up a special display area, including a Christmas tree with book ornaments. For the spring book fair, she makes certain the display includes books from the Summer Recommended Reading Lists. These lists are for students entering middle school and for students moving into high school. The fair gives students and parents the opportunity to purchase many of the books the students will need to read over the summer. Karen emphasizes that using two companies for her book fairs provides a larger variety of titles.

❋ *Kathleen Yaeger, Neshaminy Middle School, Neshaminy School District, Langhorne, Pennsylvania*

"Book Fair Tip"

Kathleen adds interest to her book fair by giving students an opportunity to win a book. During the morning announcements, she asks a question that students can try to answer. She then posts the question near the library entrance. For example, her question may relate to the history of books, the Newbery Medal, or a pseudonym used by an author. The answer can be determined only on the day of the question, and students must use a reference in the library to determine the correct answer. The first student to submit the correct answer can select a book from the fair or use the dollar amount toward a book of higher value. Kathleen reveals that day's winner during afternoon announcements.

Displays and Bulletin Boards to Promote Reading

Charleen Koppi, Rosemount Middle School, Independent School District 196 (Rosemount, Apple Valley, Eagan), Rosemount, Minnesota

"Look Who's Reading"

Rosemount Middle School's big initiative to increase the reading scores on the eighth-grade basic standards test resulted in a schoolwide program around the theme "Read and Succeed." Classroom teachers, especially reading teachers, heavily emphasized the theme in their curriculum.

Media specialist Char Koppi became involved in the yearlong initiative when she decided to piggyback off the "Read and Succeed" theme in the media center. She chose "Look Who's Reading" as her related theme. In order to have her project ready to display in the media center for the opening day of school, Char spent several summer days photographing school staff members in a variety of settings. Regardless of the setting, they were always reading. Her goal was to present school staff members reading in a relaxed, leisurely fashion; that is one of the reasons she took most of the photos away from a school setting.

Photo 8.1. "Look Who's Reading" invites everyone in the school, including these custodial staff members, to model good reading habits and inspire students to read. ***(Rosemount Middle School, Rosemount, Minnesota, Independent School District 196)***

After photographing the teachers and staff, Char took several group photos to a copy shop and had them enlarged to 11 x 17 inches and laminated. For example, she took a photo of four custodial staff members reading (see Photo 8.1). She also took a photo of the principal and assistant principal sitting under a tree and, of course, they were reading. She then displayed these enlarged photos at the media center entrance under a large banner that read "Look Who's Reading." Char also enlarged to 8½ x 17 inches the individual photos of teaching staff and slipped them into clear acrylic freestanding frames for displaying on the tops of the bookshelves throughout the school library media center.

The project received a very positive response from staff, students, parents, and the custodians. Because of the great feedback, Char has expanded the project to include students. When she learned that a reading teacher had made arrangements for the students in a struggling eighth-grade class to read to the early childhood students once a week, Char took photos of the students reading, enlarged them to 8½ x 11 inches, and displayed them with the staff photos. This was also a big success, especially with the little four-year-old students and their eighth-grade reading partners who were invited to the media center to see their photos on display.

❋ *Nancy Caplanis, Wolfe Middle School, Center Line Public Schools, Center Line, Michigan*

"Displays of Biographical Characters in the Media Center"

Also at Wolfe Middle School, media specialist Nancy Caplanis enjoys using the media center to display students' work. For example, one of the sixth-grade classes made coffee-can busts of their favorite biographical personality after reading a book about the person. They wrapped a coffee can with colored paper and added such features as a wig, eyeglasses, and a mustache.

Events and Activities to Promote Reading and Libraries

❋ *Michele Soeder, Beachwood Middle School, Beachwood School District, Beachwood, Ohio*

"Rock, Roll & Read: A Right-to-Read Week Schoolwide Celebration"

At the middle-school level, teens get excited about activities that are relevant to their everyday lives. Each year, as a way to connect kids to reading in an enjoyable way, the state of Ohio designates one week as Right-To-Read Week. The library staff at Beachwood Middle School plans a week filled with activities including contests, booktalks, and sustained silent reading in all classes. Among the themes they've covered are music, sports, and movies.

When the Rock & Roll Hall of Fame and Museum opened in Cleveland, it gave media specialist Michele Soeder a focal point for the school's most successful Right-To-Read Week project ever. The theme "Rock, Roll & Read" allowed the flexibility to build Beachwood Middle School's own Rock & Roll Museum (inside a vacant room) housing memorabilia from the 1950s through the 1990s. Many staff members contributed personal articles for the exhibits, and every teacher donated an old photo for the display titled "When They were Young." After the "official" ribbon-cutting ceremony, students toured the Rock & Roll Museum. They delighted in seeing the school principal's letter sweater and peace sign medallion. Old toys, Barbie dolls, eight-track tapes, and a phonograph player piqued their curiosity. However, it was the full-wall display of album covers through the decades and T-shirts with slogans that drew the most attention.

To kick off the week, a speaker from the Cleveland Rock & Roll Hall of Fame and Museum came and spoke to the students about memorable rock stars he had met through his job. The students asked him many interesting questions. Students and staff also enjoyed a rock & roll contest where student singing groups competed for prizes (T-shirts from the Rock & Roll Hall of Fame). Students who completed a book that week wrote their book report on a cardboard cutout of a 45-rpm record, which was then used as part of the library display. As a culminating event, the whole school went to the movie theater to see *Mr. Holland's Opus*. (Michele notes that the school does this occasionally and that the theater usually gives the school a private morning showing at a reduced rate.)

It was a great week! Everyone got involved and had fun while learning that everyone is connected through music.

Michele emphasizes that you don't have to live near the Rock & Roll Hall of Fame to do this activity. Just find an unused classroom or storage area in your own building and turn it into your own museum. Students and staff can let their imaginations take off and have tremendous fun with this project.

Michele Soeder, Beachwood Middle School, Beachwood School District, Beachwood, Ohio

"Other Innovative Right-to-Read Ideas"

Although Michele knew it would be difficult to top the celebration described above, Beachwood has come close with other Right-To-Read Week themes. One year they built the BMS Titanic, which rivaled the excitement of the movie *Titanic*. Faces of each of the students could be seen in each of the ship's portholes, and each student aboard tried to make it into one of the lifeboats by reading. Michele noted that the students loved seeing themselves on the ship, and each morning she discovered that many faces had moved to be with their friends. (The office had duplicates of every student and staff member photo on adhesive-backed paper, which she cut out and put into every porthole. The small photos were duplicates of their I.D. pictures.) Students recorded the number of pages they read that week on Titanic tickets, wrote book reports on life preservers, and received Lifesavers® for prizes.

When the new Cleveland Browns stadium was erected, Beachwood Middle School also built its own football stadium (see Photo 8.2). Student faces filled the dog pound seating area and chocolate footballs were the delicious prizes. That year, book reports were written on cardboard cutouts of footballs and helmets.

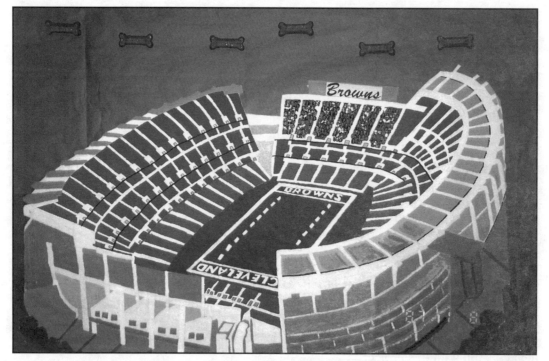

Photo 8.2. This painting of the new Cleveland Browns stadium includes students' photos in the stands and real dog biscuits overhead displaying words such as "read" and "win."
(Beachwood Middle School, Beachwood, Ohio, Beachwood School District)

Other topics have included "The Road to the White House" for the 2000 presidential election, "Go for the Gold" to celebrate the summer Olympics in Australia, and "Cleveland: All-Star City" for the bicentennial. With the release of the Harry Potter movie, Michele has decided to use Harry Potter as this year's theme. She plans to hang up a broom with Harry Potter aboard, flying across the library. To advertise Beachwood's theme, she will get a pair of Harry Potter glasses and take pictures of teachers and students wearing them while reading a book. The photographs will be enlarged to poster size and displayed in the halls under a "Caught Reading" caption. Of course, she will make sure that the principal and custodian are a part of the display. She has already started buying prizes, such as Harry Potter stationery, as she sees them or finds them on sale. For the culminating activity, she hopes that the whole school will go see the movie.

 Sandy Bernahl, F.E. Peacock Middle School, Itasca School District #10, Itasca, Illinois

"Culture of Readers"

Sandy Bernahl believes that reading promotion is important in developing a "culture of readers." The enthusiastic media specialist and the chair of the Language Arts Department at Peacock Middle School saw a need for reading promotion to be extended beyond the traditional library media settings. In their collaborative efforts to promote reading, they invited teachers and community leaders who are role models to speak to students. They found that each grade level has different needs. For example, the seventh grade wanted speakers tied in with reading and careers. The sixth grade wanted rewards and some contest components. The eighth grade wanted booktalks involving students.

Sandy weaves all of these elements into the school's reading promotion program. Community resources play an important role. For the seventh-grade classes, Sandy invited guest speakers to discuss how reading has impacted their lives and their profession. They also read a favorite selection of literature to the students. If some speakers were not sure about the interest level of their selection, they were encouraged to discuss it with the language arts chairperson. Sandy found that involving speakers from the community illustrated to the seventh graders that reading is a vital part of the culture. She discovered that the local community is rich in resource people eager to speak to students. Leaders who can relate well to the middle-school students include the mayor, the police chief, a Chicago Wolves player, a CFO of a local business, and an official from the local fire department. This program is so popular, it is held each quarter of the school year.

Sandy also recognizes the important role booktalks play in encouraging middle-school students to read. In her efforts to turn kids onto special books, she partnered with the youth librarian from the local branch of the Itasca Public Library to conduct booktalks. They present joint talks to every grade level. Over time, the booktalks have become an ongoing reading-promotion activity that continues throughout the year. For the eighth-grade classes, the two professionals read the same book, and in their booktalk they discuss the pros and cons of the topic. Following the booktalk, eighth-grade students who read the book were encouraged to join in the discussion. Sometimes teachers joined in too. With everyone's participation, it becomes a lively and educational event.

Sandy begins promoting reading as soon as school starts in the fall. She hangs flyers around the school and issues reading tickets for books read. The secretaries read announcements over the school PA system in the morning or afternoon. Sandy says that she does not want to overdo the rewards, so the reading tickets are turned in at the media center for rewards only through December. Students who read books approved by their reading teacher receive a reading ticket to be redeemed for a small piece of candy in the media center. The ticket is also put into a weekly lottery drawing for a prize at the end of the week. (Sandy has found it best to require reading teacher approval of books so that they are not reading "quickies" or "repeats" just to get a reading lottery ticket.)

Teachers keep track of the books that were read and make sure they are quality books, and Sandy is in charge of offering the rewards: sale items she buys over the summer or freebies she gathers at trade shows. Media center circulation statistics for these months are always high. The grade level that earns the most reading tickets also gets a grade-level reward, which ranges from a movie treat in the media center to having the PTO give them ice cream at lunch. Rewards vary every year.

Students especially look forward to attending the culminating all-school event, usually a performance by Urban Gateways of Chicago. This is a booking agency for many small acting groups in the Chicago area specializing in school performances. They have booked wonderful performances that are about the lives and work of such famous people as Edgar Allan Poe and Martin Luther King, Jr. The program is extended into the classroom through various follow-up activities related to language arts.

Balancing the academic requirements for all subject areas as well as providing time for speakers is very important to everyone in the school. Even though the speakers' presentations are successful annual events incorporated into the school's academic standards and programs, Sandy also wanted to include video production. With another teacher, she applied for and received a grant from the DuPage Library System (local county system) to tape an author discussing books with the Peacock Middle School students. They are currently planning to do four sessions that focus on different experts in various genres of literature. Each expert will discuss books with students to promote the love of reading. Guests will include experts from the local community as well as Illinois authors. Presentations will be recorded on a DVD disk for archiving and future duplication, and video copies will be made for public and school library checkout.

To involve the students, the Language Arts Department teachers plan to select, prepare, and practice with students before videotaping the author. Sandy stresses that video projects work better when all stakeholders are involved in the planning and execution of the project. The young adult librarian at Itasca Public Library and Sandy plan to meet with the DuPage Library System during the summer to learn about their requirements, record keeping, and timelines. The Itasca Public Library will book the author and experts and plan a video debut for the completed project. They will then meet with the chair of the Language Arts Department to plan the video recording sessions. Through the collaborative efforts of the media specialist, teachers, and public librarians, the project is on the road to success and will certainly add to Sandy's list of exciting programs that help her fulfill her major goal to create a "culture of readers" at Peacock Middle High School.

✳ Wayne Martin, Hand Middle School, Richmond School District One, Columbia, South Carolina

"Reading Is FUNdamental"

Community involvement is the key to successful reading programs at Hand Middle School in Columbia, South Carolina. During the spring semester, college athletes, a coach, parents, and even the governor of South Carolina became involved in the most recent "Reading Is FUNdamental" (RIF) program. Last year's theme, "Favorite Books of Our Favorite People," encouraged reading in the various classes that had been selected to participate in the RIF book giveaways during three distributions over a three-month period.

Each student was allowed to choose a free book to add to his or her personal collection during each of the three distributions. During the first distribution, Wayne and parent volunteers visited classrooms with carts containing RIF books. Following a discussion of the rules for entering a "Choose Your Favorite Book" poster contest, students were invited to choose a book from the cart to read and keep.

They then planned an exciting program for the second distribution of books. Members of the University of South Carolina's basketball, tennis, and golf teams visited the classrooms and read to the students from their favorite books. The athletes also shared their feelings about how reading had been an important influence in their lives and education. Following the presentations, parent volunteers invited the students to choose a second book from the carts filled with "RIF giveaways."

During the final distribution of "RIF giveaways," the students chose from the RIF carts while Martin held a drawing to choose one student from each participating class to attend a very special event in April along with the top Accelerated Reader point earners.

For the April event, South Carolina Governor Jim Hodges visited the media center and read to the top Accelerated Reader students and the students who were chosen in the drawing. For about 25 minutes he read excerpts and discussed passages from one of the Harry Potter books. He also presented gift certificates (for the spring book fair) to the winners of the poster contest. All students at Hand Middle School were able to enjoy the celebrity visit, as the event was broadcast throughout the school through the closed-circuit TV system. After his presentation, the governor was guest of honor at a reception in the media center where he visited with students and posed for pictures with them.

Noreen L. Shannon, Jackson Intermediate School, Pasadena Independent School District, Pasadena, Texas

"Wildcat Reader Club"

Students at Jackson Intermediate School look forward to becoming a member of the "Wildcat Reader Club." To begin the process, the reading teacher submits the eligible student's name to library media specialist Noreen Shannon. In response, Noreen sends an envelope containing a letter that explains the program (they must earn 100 reading points to be a Wildcat) and welcomes the student into membership in the club. The envelope also includes ice-cream coupons and a Wildcat identification item for the student. Identification items depend on how the media specialist circulates the materials. (Noreen notes: Until the students were required to wear photo I.D.'s, the Wildcat Reader received a special library card which changed in design and color each year for the three-year intermediate cycle. For a while they received Wildcat spirit pins, but the backs broke off easily and the pins had to be replaced too often. Now she uses a Wildcat spirit sticker that can be placed easily on the back of the I.D. badge.)

In April, she recognizes the Wildcat Readers in some special way. Sometimes the reading department and the library hold a theme dinner for the readers and their parents. Each reader receives a certificate, a popular book, and a pen. When the budget does not stretch that far, the library media center staff hosts a breakfast for the Wildcat Readers and their reading teachers. They cover the tables with tablecloths and decorate them. Then they put a special gift book at each honored reader's place setting. The event concludes with the principal giving each student a certificate. A parent volunteer takes a picture of each presentation for the students to keep. For a unique twist, one year Noreen invited students to hunt for Easter eggs filled with candy and money.

To organize such a club, you can be flexible, as the criteria and procedures depend upon each school's reading and library programs. At Jackson Intermediate, the program begins anew each year with students required to earn their 100 points again.

✳ *Nancy Caplanis, Wolfe Middle School, Center Line Public Schools, Center Line, Michigan*

"Battle of the Books"

Sixth and seventh graders at Wolfe Middle School enjoy reading during a special program, "Battle of the Books." Teams are given up to three clues for points; they have to name the title of the book, plus they get an extra point for knowing the author. The sixth-grade students have four shelves of books to cover in a 12-week period. There are eight titles (multiple copies) to a shelf, and they are encouraged to read as many as they can from their shelf in a three-week period. There are two classes assigned to a shelf, and the classes switch shelves every three weeks.

The media center sponsors preliminary battles in the media center between the classes using "buzzers and bells," and a final battle with the two top teams. The first-place team wins a pizza party for its class, and the second-place team wins an ice-cream party for its class. It becomes very competitive, but the students read books they might not otherwise check out from the library.

The seventh grade "Battle of the Books" primarily works the same way, but they have three shelves of books that rotate every three weeks instead of four. Their final battle is held in the school cafeteria, and the entire seventh grade is invited to watch. The media specialist chooses two 8-member teams from each class to participate, and the winning teams get the following rewards:

- First place wins a pizza party for the class.

- Second place wins an ice-cream party for the class.

- Third place wins a candy bar of choice for the whole class.

During the past year, five seventh graders read all 24 books. They will each get a $25 gift certificate to a bookstore for their accomplishments.

✳ *Kathleen Yaeger, Neshaminy Middle School, Neshaminy School District, Langhorne, Pennsylvania*

"Reading Olympics"

Throughout the state of Pennsylvania, students are encouraged to voluntarily participate in the "Reading Olympics." The program is designed to entice students to read and requires teacher and librarian collaboration. Each county provides a list of books, and all middle-school students have the same reading list. Teams are put together, and each team decides on a name. Students read and prepare for the Olympic match, which includes questions formulated by a special panel. An evening is chosen for the contest, and students and parents are invited to a designated school where teams compete against each other. There is a moderator and a scorekeeper, and almost everyone goes away with some sort of ribbon. The media specialists, teachers, parents, and students eagerly await the "Reading Olympics" each year.

❋ *Noreen L. Shannon, Jackson Intermediate School, Pasadena Independent School District, Pasadena, Texas*

"Booktalks"

Noreen gets a resounding response after sending the following notice to all teachers:

MEMO:

Memo from the Media Center

"I am ready to do brief booktalks on subjects of your choice. Come talk with me about your topic and length of available time. I am willing to bring the talk to your room, or I will present it in the library."

Library Resources and Skills

❋ *Judy Koehl, Haggard Middle School, Plano Independent School District, Plano, Texas*

"Library Advisory Board"

Media specialist Judy Koehl established the Haggard Middle School Library Advisory Board to provide students in sixth, seventh, and eighth grades with an opportunity to attend regular meetings and promote the media center. Judy invites students in all grades to inform her if they are interested in a board position. (Any student indicating an interest is usually appointed to the board.) During the meetings, members of the "Advisory Board" talk about books they recently read, recommend titles, and share ideas about books. Some board members bring other students to the meetings to discuss books. Some board members even bring friends to the library to show them around and recommend books.

The Advisory Board sometimes takes part in fund-raising projects to fund special programs or activities related to the media center. Last February, they sold Mardi Gras beads to help partially fund a school mural. Student advisory board members attend special activities during the school year. For example, they enjoy lunch in the media center several times. In December Judy makes gingerbread and invites the board members to decorate the gingerbread while the group discusses books.

✳ *Nancy Caplanis, Wolfe Middle School, Center Line Public Schools, Center Line, Michigan*

"Library Orientation"

Each fall the media center sponsors a library orientation for students. The new sixth-grade students are given a walking tour of Wolfe Middle School Media Center by media specialist Nancy Caplanis. They learn the rules of the library as well as where specific materials are located. Within several weeks, they are invited back to learn how to use the electronic catalog. At this time, they are given an assignment related to using the library and electronic catalog, and they are told to turn it in for a language arts grade. Seventh and eighth graders also attend a library orientation where they review information they learned during the previous year.

During the year, students in grades six and seven are given lessons on using almanacs, special dictionaries, special encyclopedias, and atlases. They are also taught how to write a book review. As an introduction, they are given examples of reviews for books that readers liked as well as those that readers did not like. After writing their own reviews, students are excited to see their reviews published.

✳ *Eileen Neill, Deer Creek Middle School, Jefferson County Public Schools, Little-ton, Colorado*

"Enrichment Lab"

The Enrichment Lab at Deer Creek Middle School is a small room adjacent to the library that contains six networked computers. Any eighth-grade student is welcome to use the lab provided they have established a research topic and a final product with their language arts teacher and the librarian.

The students brainstorm ideas that they want to research and, after discussion with their teacher, choose one topic to research extensively. The teacher provides the student with a library pass to use the enrichment lab. (If a teacher is re-teaching a lesson or introducing a new topic that the student has already mastered, this often becomes the time that the student visits the lab.) Consequently, students might come to the lab once a week, once a month, or just for a couple of days in a row. The time frame is flexible, and it varies depending on each project.

Students have researched slavery in Sudan, the future of aircraft design, and the cons of standardized testing. One student who researched presidential elections chose to present a presidential speech as her final project. A special box is available for each student in the library where he or she can leave research notes and articles, and the media specialist adds to the box any articles that she finds relating to the student's topic. The final product can be on paper, a PowerPoint presentation, a polished speech, or any mutually agreed-upon product.

Eileen finds that students involved in the program have shown great enthusiasm for their topics. They enjoy the privilege of working independently and gain advanced research skills in the process. Throughout the year she enjoys having the one-on-one contact and seeing the various projects through from beginning to end.

✳ *Kathleen Yaeger, Neshaminy Middle School, Neshaminy School District, Langhorne, Pennsylvania*

"Student Book Reviews"

Peer recommendations enhance student interest in reading and help students at Neshaminy Middle School select the books they want to read. The student book review is a popular way to give students a list of favorite titles to read over the summer. Before the project begins, Kathleen introduces the idea and shares the lesson in a mini workshop for teachers. She then provides the students with a review form to complete. She and the teacher share information about book reviewing with students, and provide sample book reviews by experts as well as former students. Although Kathleen usually handles her program through the English classes, it can work in most any discipline.

Student reviews are divided into three categories: (1) fiction, (2) nonfiction, and (3) biography. Each entry includes the title, author, and a brief annotation. The student's name and grade level are listed at the end of the review. When the students complete their reviews, the library staff collects them and edits them as little as possible so as not to change the main entry.

If several students write a review of the same book, Kathleen and her staff select the best written annotation for print and list the book as a favorite. They then add that title to a special list of favorite authors and titles included in the final product: an attractive review booklet given to all participating students. The cover is specially designed using a catchy title and graphics on bright paper.

When the booklets are ready for production, Kathleen sends a sample to the district copy center where the booklets are copied and collated according to Kathleen's instructions. Students eagerly pick up the booklets at the end of school to use for summer reading. She uses catchy titles for the booklets, such as "Shades of Summer Reading" and "Sizzling Summer Reading."

Next year, before the summer vacation, Kathleen plans to put a partial list of the recommended book reviews on the school Web site under "Library News." When school resumes in September, the list will be updated. This project may be ongoing throughout the year and updated at regular intervals.

Following are examples of student book reviews by students at Neshaminy Middle School:

B-BAR Barkley, Charles-THE OUTRAGEOUS CHARLES BARKLEY. If you like basketball, then this book is for you. It describes where Charles grew up and his early life with a full picture section in the middle of the book. The book gives an in-depth report into Charles' career. Recommended by David Smith, grade 9.

616.96 FOR Ford, Michael Thomas—100 QUESTIONS AND ANSWERS ABOUT AIDS. I used this book for my research paper and it helped me a lot. There was a lot of information which was easy to read and was up to date. It's a good book to read just to learn and get more information about AIDS and HIV. Recommended by Bill Jones, grade 9.

✺ *Eileen Neill, Deer Creek Middle School, Jefferson County Public Schools, Littleton, Colorado*

"Book Reviews"

The book review database is accessed via the Deer Creek Middle School Home page (http://204.98/1.2/midle/deercreek/) under "Research Tools." When a student is in a quandary for a good book, this database offers an excellent place to start. Books can be accessed by title, author, number of pages, or genre. Frequently, students just browse through the entries looking for a book that appeals to them. The database contains a short summary of the book, the reviewer names, comments such as, "I loved/hated this book because . . . ," and a 1- to 5-star rating. Students enjoy using the database for recommendations because the books are reviewed by their peers; quite often by students they know. The book reviews are edited and collected in various eighth-grade language arts classes. They are brought to the library where two student assistants enter them into the database. The software used is *Claris Home Page* and *Filemaker Pro*.

✺ *Nancy Caplanis, Wolfe Middle School, Center Line Public Schools, Center Line, Michigan*

"Trivial Pursuit Reference Challenge"

The eighth grade participates in the Trivial Pursuit Reference Challenge. This is a weeklong exercise per class where students learn about many different types of reference books and then answer questions. Each class is divided into four-person teams, and each team is responsible for 60 questions. They learn to use some seldom-used reference books like the *Visual Dictionary*, or *Famous First Facts*, and *Facts About the Presidents*. Using indexes becomes a priority to mastering the assignment.

Media specialist Nancy Caplanis finds that even the most reluctant learner usually excels by becoming a "reference detective." Kids with a great deal of energy or short attention spans are often the first to finish and help their teammates. When the top team from each block class is determined, that team then competes against another middle school in the area. The winning school gets its name engraved on the trophy, which they keep for that school year. Nancy notes that this competition is very detailed and somewhat difficult, but very challenging. All the top classes from both schools enjoy a pizza party together.

Shakespeare and Poetry

✳ *Karen Paulus, First Colony Middle School, Fort Bend Independent School District, Sugar Land, Texas*

"Troupe de Jour"

Collaborative efforts between media specialist Karen Paulus and the eighth-grade reading teacher at First Colony Middle School resulted in a full-day campus visit by Troupe de Jour, which provided students with an opportunity to see Shakespeare's plays come alive. Students were immersed in the magic of Shakespeare when two actors gave a 45-minute presentation to each group of students. They talked about life during the Elizabethan period, described what plays were like during that time, and even demonstrated sword fighting. One of the highlights of the presentation was a modern-day language play of *Romeo and Juliet* acted out by the students. Volunteer student participants are provided a script and time to practice before presenting. The response to the presentation was overwhelming by both teachers and students. (Note: Although Troupe de Jour is a Texas-based company, media specialists in other states may find similar companies available in their own states.)

Storytelling

✳ *Cindy Reinhart, South Oldham Middle School, Oldham County Schools, Crestwood, Kentucky*

"Urban Legends Storytelling Festival"

Media specialist Cindy Reinhart says that the most important aspect of storytelling for young adults is story selection, and one type of story that will appeal to almost all young adults is the urban legend. Therefore, Cindy collaborated with the seventh-grade language arts teachers at South Oldham Middle School and the local elementary school to develop an exciting program, "Legends from the Burbs: A Slightly Suburban Twist to the Urban Legend." Cindy introduced the seventh-grade students to the urban legend by telling one of her favorite urban legends. She also discussed the oral tradition and how the stories evolved over time. Students were particularly interested to find out that the stories

abound on the Internet and in the movies. Classroom teachers discussed the following topics with students:

- Purpose of a legend

- Most popular themes in legends

- Why we like to be scared

- Techniques the writer uses to build anxiety and anticipation

Following the discussion, students brainstorm possible topics, plots, settings, and
characters for their own urban legends (e.g., disappearing teachers; strange lunchroom
food; strange creatures in the air-conditioning duct). Students are then asked to write their
stories and share them orally. Teachers encourage the creative process by using the following steps:

- Pre-write legend

- Develop a rough draft

- Conference with a peer

- Revise

- Conference with the teacher or media specialist

- Revise again

- Edit

- Publish (share with elementary students; bound volume of stories in media center)

Each day a special period is set aside when the classroom lights are turned out and
students have time to read or tell their legends. The creative works are also bound into book
form and placed in the media center collection.

Excited fifth graders from the local elementary school are invited to the "Storytelling
Festival" at South Oldham Middle School. The festival is held in the media center, which is
set up to appear spooky and somewhat haunted because the event is planned for the end of
October. The seventh-grade storytellers dress and decorate their special area to reflect the
urban legend they are sharing.

Cindy recommends the following Web sites for educators who need more information about urban legends:

The Urban Legends Reference Pages: http://www.snopes2.com (accessed 05/02/02)

Urban Legends and Folklore: http://urbanlegends.about.com (accessed 05/02/02)

She also recommends the following books written by Jan Harold Burnvand:

The Choking Doberman And Other "New" Urban Legends

Curses! Broiled Again!: The Hottest Legends Going

Too Good to be True: The Colossal Book of Urban Legends

The Vanishing Hitchhiker: American Urban Legends and Their Meanings

Curriculum:
Beyond English/Language Arts

Health

✳ *Maureen Luebbers, Russell Middle School, Millard Public Schools, Omaha, Nebraska*

"What's Up Doc: Discovering Diseases"

A collaboration between the media specialist and the health teacher at Russell Middle School in Omaha, Nebraska, resulted in a more meaningful and challenging health unit that focused on diseases and included a research project for seventh graders. The unit was based on a pilot project that used health curriculum to create a learning atmosphere and a final product that looks very different from the typical encyclopedia-based paper-and-pen report. Students involved in the pilot project provided suggestions that gave a great deal of insight into their learning styles and showed how they wanted to share the information gained through research. Based upon the suggestions gathered in class, students will design their course of study by

1. Selecting topics from personal perspectives and discussion and involving their parents in their choices.

2. Using magazine and newspaper articles (*ProQuest* and *Gale Research Health Module*) to research current information on inherited diseases.

3. Interviewing health professionals, friends, or family members who may have information to share concerning the selected topic.

4. Creating projects using multimedia (*HyperStudio*, PowerPoint, *iMovie*). Projects could involve creating a brochure or a poster display.

5. Sharing the results with their peers and the community by placing projects such as poster displays or brochures in doctors' offices.

The health unit was integrated into other curricula areas through activities such as the following:

Health

Because students will tackle assignments they consider relevant or meaningful, they are asked to select a disease that impacts them personally. One boy commented that his family was going to adopt a baby from Romania. They already knew that the baby had a cardiac problem, so he decided to investigate her condition so that he could be more understanding of her needs.

Parents who are health professionals volunteered to talk to kids about what they do. Some offered to display in their offices the brochures and posters that the students produced. This community involvement promotes positive relations between the school and community.

Language Arts

One language arts assignment requires students to research a topic and produce a piece of nonfiction writing. They can also present mini-lessons on selecting topics, finding and evaluating information, taking notes, and organizing their ideas.

Technology

Technology is embedded in this project from the time they model where to find information, to the programs used to construct the projects, and finally, to sharing the presentations.

Communication Skills

One suggested activity is to interview a health professional, someone in research, or a family member. Some students videotaped the interview and used segments in multimedia projects. Maureen has found that projects such as these move students beyond the typical learning experiences and better prepare them for high school and college.

Social Studies and Science

Wayne Martin, Hand Middle School, Richmond School District One, Columbia, South Carolina

"History Day"

At Hand Middle School, Wayne and the social studies teachers collaborated on a special program that culminated in a special "History Day." Seventh-grade students were assigned a project through their social studies classes. The projects were to be based on the theme, "Pioneers of the Past," which could focus on famous people or events. Examples of project topics included various battles of World War II, the Korean War, Pearl Harbor, Chuck Yeager, Amelia Earhart, the Wright Brothers, and Albert Einstein. Throughout the planning process, Wayne played an important role in assisting teachers and supplying resources from the media center, the district interlibrary loan system, and the award-winning Richland County Public Library.

Some students chose to develop their presentations as a video production. Using the television production center located in the media center, Wayne helped them produce their projects. These 10-minute presentations were combinations of Microsoft PowerPoint, video clips (both current and historical footage), historical audio selections, and graphics and pictures from various Internet sites. They all included voice-over narration by students.

On the specially designated "History Day," all the projects were displayed up and down the hallways and in the media center. They were divided into special categories such as documentaries, essays, video productions, and storyboards. Wayne also invited a panel of judges (the principal, a history teacher, a college professor, and a parent) to determine award recipients.

The winner at Hand Middle School, whose project focused on Albert Einstein, went on to become the South Carolina state winner. That win enabled the student to attend the National History Day competition in Washington along with one of the teachers.

�֎ *Brian Joseph, Neptune Middle School, Osceola County, Kissimmee, Florida*

"Voyager Florida Fling"

Media specialist Brian Joseph and classroom teacher Joy Penney-Wieter developed a six-week unit on Florida for seventh graders. The project was tied to the Makison Island restoration project and included a field trip to collect shark teeth at the beach.

To develop the project, they initiated or completed the following steps:

1. Classes brainstormed possible Florida topics and students selected their own topic for research.

2. They developed a timeline and wrote a contract about completing the project for students, parents, and teachers to sign.

3. Students composed 10 questions that would guide them in researching their topic.

4. During the next two weeks, the teachers encouraged students to use the Internet in the classroom, media center, or at home.

5. Brian loaned resources and materials on the selected topics to the various classrooms.

6. After two weeks of research, students were required to turn in a list with a minimum of three or four resources they used to find information on the topics.

7. For their final projects, students had to include a three- to five-page report, the answers to their 10 questions, and a visual display related to the topic. (While many used a tri-fold board, some students used computer applications such as *Hyperstudio* to develop their displays. Some cooked food as part of the display. One student brought a Florida turtle as an animal guest.)

8. On presentation day, students rotated through the media center where they shared information on their topic, or judged other projects and presentations. To reduce the number of students in the school library media center at one time, Brian scheduled Florida Storytellers (staff members on campus) to tell stories about Florida to groups of students circulating through classrooms as well. (Brian sometimes uses the list of storytellers at the county library as a resource.)

The event was so successful, and the student feedback was so positive, the media specialist has already begun planning and expanding the project for next year.

Technology and Communications

✳ *Wayne Martin, Hand Middle School, Richmond School District One, Columbia, South Carolina*

"Broadcast News"

In addition to being the library media specialist at Hand Middle School, Wayne also teaches an elective video production class, which is limited to eight students. In the course, students gain a wealth of knowledge related to broadcasting such as

- Using a digital camera
- Scanning photos, video tape
- Integrating CD and video clips
- Mixing

Each morning, students in the class prepare and present the news, weather, and sports on the daily program broadcast throughout the school over closed-circuit television. Part of the broadcast is videotaped, and part is presented live. Every Monday, students are in for a special treat when "Principal's Corner" is broadcast throughout the school. The principal often welcomes the students as she sits in a rocking chair in the media center. She is then videotaped for four to five minutes as she highlights special events in the school and focuses on news items such as sports, safety issues, or special classroom projects. The video may be set on the physical education (PE) field, in the art room, or any other location where campus events are taking place.

✳ *Nancy Caplanis, Wolfe Middle School, Center Line Public Schools, Center Line, Michigan*

"Wolfe Video Production Team"

Wolfe Middle School students in Center Line, Michigan, enjoy a broadcast in their classrooms each morning. A team of three eighth graders and two seventh graders run the morning announcements through a school-wide broadcast. Media specialist Nancy

Caplanis and a dedicated faculty member, Dave Roman, teach the young people how to do such things as videotape; mix sound; and run the board, cameras, and lights.

For a few minutes during the first hour of class each morning, the principal or assistant principal reads the announcements with a guest host. (Each week a different student is selected as the guest host.) In their announcement they focus on a variety of items. They usually provide a quick review of the day's happenings. They may also recognize special students, announce upcoming events, or give scores for sporting events.

Personal Interests

Art

Nancy Caplanis, Wolfe Middle School, Center Line Public Schools, Center Line, Michigan

"Displays of Student Work in the Media Center"

At Wolfe Middle School, media specialist Nancy Caplanis encourages teachers to use the media center to display students' work. The art teacher frequently takes her up on this offer and uses the library to display various types of student art ranging from jewelry to sculpture. By adding a learning component, Nancy makes it a program.

Career Choices

Diane O. Davis and Nancy C. Owen, Harry F. Byrd Middle School, Henrico County Public Schools, Richmond, Virginia

"Career Education"

The career education resources provide the students at Byrd Middle School in Richmond, Virginia, with the opportunity to investigate skills and abilities required for various occupations. The more students know about themselves and the world of work, the more likely they will make better decisions about their future. All students can explore a large variety of potential job opportunities. They see the relationship and importance of their school subjects and the world of work. It connects the next most important link—the transition from middle school to high school.

For this topic, Diane invites all teachers to schedule classes in the school library media center for planned career-research opportunities. Some classes may do a career exploration. Other classes may do more advanced study. The Family and Living Studies classes visit actual work sites and engage in "job shadowing." The students in the eighth-grade gifted program complete career research and identify colleges with programs for their choices. All career resources are located together to create a "career center." Some of the activities include:

- Doing a career inventory or career plan to define interests and abilities

- Researching job choices from current computer software programs, pamphlets, books, and the Internet

- Designing advertisements and business cards for occupations

- Assembling a list of local employers, providing job descriptions of what they do, and preparing oral reports with visuals

Games and Puzzles

✵ *Nancy Caplanis, Wolfe Middle School, Center Line Public Schools, Center Line, Michigan*

"Challenging the Mind Through Games and Puzzles"

Because she also appreciates the value of games and puzzles in developing critical thinking and good sportsmanship, Nancy encourages students to visit the media center before school, after school, and during lunch hours. (They are allowed 30 students on a special media pass for each lunch hour.) During that time they can read or browse or play games and puzzles. Fifteen spatial relations puzzles are available, all lined up in little baskets on the circulation desk. For every three puzzles students complete, they get a piece of candy. The puzzles challenge all levels of students in the school ranging from the special education students to the gifted students.

Chess, checkers, and tic-tac-toe games are also available to challenge the young minds (see Photo 8.3). In fact, these have become so popular that Nancy has numbered the sets and put the pieces in plastic containers. Students are asked to sign up for a game by number, and they become responsible for the set while they play. This policy has streamlined game use and eliminated having extra pawns in any one set. Chess is so popular at Wolfe Middle School that the library media center has about thirty chess sets available for students and for use by the Chess Club. Thanks to the emphasis on mind-stretching games, membership in the Chess Club has risen from 12 members to 52.

The Chess Club meets on Wednesdays after school for 10 weeks. Students learn good sportsmanship by knowing the opponent's name and shaking hands after each game to congratulate the winner. A tournament is held each year to determine the Wolfe Middle School champion, and certificates are given to each grade winner as a bonus.

Photo 8.3. Students like these chess club members develop critical thinking skills by participating in game tournaments in the school library media center. *(Wolfe Middle School, Center Line, Michigan, Center Line Public Schools)*

Interesting People and Things

Nancy Caplanis, Wolfe Middle School, Center Line Public Schools, Center Line, Michigan

"Brown Bag Lunch Seminars"

At Wolfe Middle School, the media center is host to various brown-bag seminars throughout the school year. Nancy invites a guest to present something of interest to students while they eat their lunch in the school library media center. Examples of favorite lunch guests include

- A veterinary technician who brought an iguana and taught reptile care
- The mother of a student who talked about caving as a hobby or vacation and brought her equipment
- A representative from the Federal Reserve who brought in bags of shredded money for the students to see

- Ringo, a monkey for the physically impaired who works for the Helping Hands organization
- A Paws for a Cause guide dog
- Clowns
- Magicians
- Storytellers
- A sports photographer
- Karate master
- A caricaturist
- A local news celebrity and meteorologist

Holidays and Special Days

❋ *Wayne Martin, Hand Middle School, Richmond School District One, Columbia, South Carolina*

"Grandmother's Day"

Each month, students eagerly await the guest reader of this special event. Wayne sends out letters asking for volunteers. A grandmother is invited to visit the media center and read a book of her choice or tell a story during the time when the grandchild's class is in the media center. Many variations on this idea could work, including "Mother's Day," "Grandfather's Day," or "Father's Day."

❋ *Noreen L. Shannon, Jackson Intermediate School, Pasadena Independent School District, Pasadena, Texas*

"Holiday Traditions"

Noreen involves faculty members and students when developing her holiday displays. She invites you to create a form and distribute it to all your faculty and staff members. Ask them to complete it by filling in the information about their favorite holiday traditions. She also suggests that you have the forms available for the students to complete and put in a basket in the library. After receiving the completed forms, type the information about the favorite holiday tradition and include the person's name. Place it on an appropriate background such as a wreath for Christmas.

Next to each description of holiday traditions she also places a related book or video cover that suits the occasion. For example, when one teacher wrote about her family's tradition of making Christmas gifts for family members, which she continues to do with her daughter, Noreen placed this tradition next to a book on Christmas crafts. This program works wonderfully at the end of November, because you may use the information for

December displays. With so many holidays at this time of year, you have many interesting traditions to explore. Best of all, library patrons keep checking out the display items.

Marney Welmers, Tortolita Middle School, Marana Unified School District, Tucson, Arizona

"Happy Birthday, Dr. Seuss"

As much as middle school students want to feel grown up, they are still kids at heart who enjoy being exposed to children's literature. The National Education Association's *Read Across America Day* celebrates Dr. Seuss's birthday on March 2 by providing all students at Tortolita Middle School the opportunity to become involved in a variety of activities.

Because part of the goal is to raise funds for the library club, Books and Beyond, to use for purchasing new books, posters, plants, and beanbag chairs, the celebration begins early. With special permission from the administrators, students are allowed to wear *Cat in the Hat* hats, a special version of which the library aide produces for the group to sell (see Photo 8.4). Appropriately clad club members man the electric frying pans and produce "green eggs and ham" wrapped in tortillas to sell to the always-hungry hordes as they arrive at school.

Photo 8.4. To support Read Across America Day, students and faculty at Tortolita Middle School celebrate Dr. Seuss's birthday with read alouds from his popular works.
(Tortolita Middle School, Maran Unified School District, Tucson, Arizona)

In the days leading up to March 2, one of the science teachers prowls the halls with a video camera and a Seuss book in hand, busily taping everyone—maintenance, office, and cafeteria workers as well as principals, teachers, students, and parents—as each reads a line from the selected volume. The film is a fun and fitting opening for the day when it is shown in all the classrooms following the morning announcements and news.

Each year, the media specialist plans a variety of contests and challenges for students. Examples of the contests and activities include

- A Dr. Seuss Trivia Contest that challenges students to use their Internet and reference skills

- An essay and drawing competition illustrating; for example, the places you'll go

- A door-decorating contest asking classes to select and illustrate a favorite "Suessism"

The library club always has new ideas and inspirations. Similarly, teachers discover innovative and relevant ways to incorporate Dr. Seuss's writings into their lesson plans with activities such as character studies or plot analyses, mini-lessons based on *The Butter Battle*, or discussions of environmental issues centered on *The Lorax*.

Throughout the day, the media center is open for an ongoing "Read-In," complete with Goldfish® crackers in honor of *One Fish, Two Fish* and Trader Joe's Cat Cookies in honor of the Cat himself. During this "Read-In," everyone has the opportunity to pick up a favorite book from those on display and entertain an eager audience with his or her best read-aloud rendition of one of Seuss's classics. Because the media center has all the books, many of them in Spanish, anyone who wants to join in can feel comfortable and appreciated. Many notable theatrical talents have been discovered as the shyest and boldest volunteers take a turn in reading to whatever group is assembled.

Certain classes choose to go off campus for part of the day and read to children at one of the nearby elementary or preschools. One group even shares the day with both youngsters and senior citizens by picking up a group of third graders and taking the show on the road to an assisted living facility. The appeal of Dr. Seuss's books to all ages makes them extra special for these community activities.

All in all, the combination of food and fun, the chance to be a kid again along with everyone else, and the invitation to remember and share make Dr. Seuss's birthday celebration one of Tortolita Middle School's most popular traditions.

For more information about Dr. Seuss and his birthday celebration, Marney suggests that you visit the following Web sites:

www.randomhouse.com/seussville (accessed 05/02/02)

www.nea.org/readacross (accessed 05/02/02)

�֍ *American Library Association, Chicago, Illinois*

"ALA Calendar of Events"

The American Library Association has an entire calendar of events to promote libraries and literacy. For complete information about the programs sponsored by ALA, telephone 1-800-545-2433 or access ALA's Web site at www.ala.org/events/promoevents. ALA can send you a packet filled with ideas for programs in your school library media center.

PROGRAMS FOR FACULTY

Programs designed around curriculum, technology, information retrieval skills, and personal interests can be as worthwhile for teachers as they are for students. Curriculum-based programs for faculty members can help them discover new teaching strategies, find worthwhile resources, and even share innovative ideas. Because teachers will all be at different skills levels concerning technology, hosting programs that enhance those skills can benefit everyone. Some library media specialists host different sessions to meet participants' beginner, intermediate, or advanced skill levels. Others host more general sessions, and allow beginners to partner up with advanced participants.

Remember also that teachers would benefit from updates on information retrieval and other skills that you use regularly but that they encounter only periodically. The more competent they feel in the school library media center, the more likely they are to bring in classes, and the more guidance they can give students while there.

Available Resources

✖ *Charleen Koppi, Rosemount Middle School, Independent School District 196 (Rosemount, Apple Valley, Eagan), Rosemount, Minnesota*

"Book News from the Media Center"

A favorite media center event for Char is the arrival of new books. She loves working with them and paging through them. Because of her classroom-teaching background, she inevitably comes up with ways that she would use some of the new titles in the classroom. As a result, she decided to find a way to share some of her ideas with faculty members.

A simple flyer called "Book News from the Media Center" seemed like a quick way to make teachers aware of new materials and to share some of her suggestions for their use. Although she distributes the flyer intermittently, Char finds that it is an excellent way to get information out in a timely manner.

❀ *Wayne Martin, Hand Middle School, Richmond School District One, Columbia, South Carolina*

"Newsletter for Teachers"

Wayne also sponsors the *Media Memo*, a newsletter to teachers that he distributes every two weeks. The information he shares includes

- Internet Web sites of interest
- New books in the media center
- Events in the media center
- *Accelerated Reader* winners for the month

❀ *Miriam A. Wiese, Mesa Verde Middle School, Poway Unified School District, San Diego, California*

"Library Open House"

Each year, Miriam Wiese hosts a Library Open House to display all the wonderful materials that have been added to the library collection. Throughout the year, as materials come in, she tags them as open-house materials so she can easily retrieve them for the open house in the spring.

Several weeks before the open house, she places flyers throughout the school advertising the event. She also publicizes it on the school calendar, posts invitations to it on the school Web site, sends e-mail reminders to all staff, and sends individual invitations to district personnel, school board members, and others in the district. Decorations for the open house include posters promoting reading as well as bookmarks that she orders for this celebration.

Miriam displays materials throughout the Mesa Verde Middle School library media center, and keeps them divided according to genre. This year she divided displays into the following groups: science, social studies, literature, general interest, professional resources, best books for children 9–12, best books for young adult readers, and new videos. Miriam prepares bibliographies of the new materials on display and makes them available for the attendees.

Teachers usually visit the displays during their prep time, and they enjoy viewing all the newest materials to determine what they might want to use. Miriam places a notepad beside each display for the teachers to take notes or to make a request for materials they would like to preview in depth at another time.

To increase attendance, she makes finger foods and drinks available throughout the day. At the entrance to the library, she has people sign in and receive raffle tickets for various prizes. Because of its informational and social value, faculty members look forward to the open house each year. As a courtesy, Miriam videotapes the event and makes it immediately available to anyone unable to attend.

✳ *Noreen L. Shannon, Jackson Intermediate School, Pasadena Independent School District, Pasadena, Texas*

"Library Open House"

Two or three weeks after the opening of school each year, Noreen hosts an open house for staff and faculty members. By that time, she believes teachers have begun to feel comfortable with their classes and lesson planning. Noreen sends an invitation to each staff member personally and schedules the event on a Friday. As a special treat for teachers, Noreen does not circulate books or schedule classes on that day so that teachers can use her open house as a respite from a busy week.

Individual table displays showcase each subject area and contain samples of student fiction and informational books, reference materials, and professional books as well as videos and kits that are related to the subject areas. On each table is a bibliography of new material.

Noreen also highlights technology by inviting teachers to visit computer stations and peruse new CD programs as well as special Internet research sites. In addition, she showcases print Internet resource guides such as *Web Feet*.

In another display area, she arranges free items such as out-of-date periodicals, posters, book covers, catalogs, and bookmarks. She allows teachers to select items and take them to their classrooms.

Added treats include good food and prizes. Food is always important at these occasions, and because Noreen enjoys cooking, she provides many pastries as well as fruit and vegetable trays. She also serves coffee and lemonade. Faculty members always look forward to the special drawing for gifts including thesauri, educational books, and packages of stickers.

The popular open house gives teachers an opportunity to socialize and learn about the new materials in the media center. The positive PR for the media center is tremendous, and the event helps solidify a special rapport between teachers and the media specialist.

Planning Session

✳ *Cindy Reinhart, South Oldham Middle School, Oldham County Schools, Crestwood, Kentucky*

"Collaborative Lunch"

In an effort to build community spirit with the faculty members at her school, once a month Cindy invites a different grade level to lunch in the South Oldham Middle School Media Center. The luncheon, funded by book fines and book fair proceeds, is held during one of the 90-minute planning periods for teachers rather than during the regular 22-minute lunch period. Lunch is ordered from local restaurants and delivered to the media center.

Once lunch has been enjoyed, the media center staff introduces a selected unit of study, and the staff and teachers work to plan the unit. Sample units include

August	6th grade	*Integrated Studies/How to Use the Library*
September	7th grade	*Storytelling/Urban Legends*
October	8th grade	*Colonial Crafts*

Promoting Reading Among Teachers

�֍ *International Reading Association (IRA)*

"Teachers as Readers"

Media specialists across the nation have developed a successful professional growth program for teachers based on the "Teachers as Readers" program initiated by the IRA. The program encourages educators to read books and provides an opportunity for sharing and discussing them. Each group should consist of an administrator, teachers, and the media specialist. You will, of course, organize your group to meet its own unique needs. The group can meet as often as the members desire, and they can meet anywhere: in restaurants, parks, homes, or at school. Some groups meet monthly; others may meet five or six times a year in the school library media center. Refreshments are usually served.

Techniques for approaching this program can vary. Participants may all read the same book, different books by the same author, or different books on a central topic. After reading the book, the group members share ideas, thoughts, and feelings as they respond to the literature. Some possible approaches are

- The group members read different young adult novels that are new to the library media center. During the session they have short discussions about how the books can be used in the classroom.

- The group members read the same young adult book, and during the session they discuss the work.

- The group focuses on a specific adult novel to read and discuss.

- The group focuses on a specific professional book to read and discuss.

The following tips will help you in establishing this excellent program:

- Purchase multiple copies with book fair proceeds, special budget appropriations through the principal, or with grant funds.

- Check with the IRA about grants to defray the cost of books provided to participants.

- Place bookplates in front of the books given to teachers to read saying that Teachers as Readers provided the books.

- Occasionally invite a guest speaker to meet with the group.

- When selecting books for the group to read, consider length, interest of topic, availability, and cost.
- Involve the school principal.

To obtain more detailed information on this program, contact the International Reading Association at 1-800-336-READ and ask for information about the "Teachers as Readers Group." A video and a starter kit are available for a fee.

Technology

Diane O. Davis and Nancy C. Owen, Harry F. Byrd Middle School, Henrico County Public Schools, Richmond, Virginia

"Tech Fest Program"

Although some staff development activities at Byrd include centrally planned experiences for teachers, most staff development takes place at different sites simultaneously. The staff development planning committee develops an initial plan for the entire year. Created because of results from a technology survey, the "Tech Fest Program" is one of many half-day programs planned during the year. During the program, teachers rotate to three different technology sessions that change each year based upon their needs.

One important facet of the program is continuous evaluation. The entire faculty evaluates each activity so suggestions can be implemented as quickly as possible. For example, evaluations from the "Tech Fest Program" were used to determine the sessions teachers could choose to attend for the next half-day inservice.

Wayne Martin, Hand Middle School, Richmond School District One, Columbia, South Carolina

"Technology Training Sessions"

Every other week, Wayne invites teachers to a technology training session. Some examples of the skills they work on are word processing, *Excel*, PowerPoint, and Internet exploration. They also learn how to access the various databases in the media center. A major focus of every training session is a brainstorming session on how to integrate technology into the classroom.

Karen Paulus, First Colony Middle School, Fort Bend Independent School District, Sugar Land, Texas

"Technology Workshops"

When new equipment and software arrive on campus, Karen Paulus immediately finds a way to share it with faculty members. She invites teachers to attend short workshops where she demonstrates the equipment or software. In small groups, teachers are given hands-on experience with the equipment during the workshop. Karen then invites teachers to use the technology in the classroom. Most recently she demonstrated the use of the Numonics Corporation's "Interactive Presentation Manager" to eager-to-learn teachers. She emphasized its practical use in the classroom.

Karen also enjoys presenting to teachers short workshops related to the Internet. One of her favorite workshops focuses on orienting new teachers on campus. She shows them how to go to the district's home page at www.fortbend.k12.tx.us/library/ and then demonstrates how to use the Web site to enrich the curriculum, determine the various materials available, and locate information about major events in the district. She also highlights various professional links that are available.

Various Ideas

"Topic Ideas for Mini-Workshops"

Media specialists from middle schools across the nation provided the following topics that have been successfully implemented into the mini-workshop format. (Mini-workshops focus on one topic, last approximately 20-30 minutes, and involve hands-on activities.)

- *Searching the Internet.* Any number of topics can be the focus of this mini-workshop. Make it a fun, interesting experience with plenty of hands-on opportunities. For example, the author Web sites in Chapter 6 could be the focus of an interesting workshop to familiarize teachers with resources available on the Internet. Teachers will enjoy sharing these sites with their students. Other workshops could highlight the community resources that also appear in Chapter 6.

- *Using the Internet for Research.* Share a variety of reference sources that can be found on the Internet. Emphasize the various search engines that are available. Ask teachers to bring a list of their favorite sites to share, and compile these into a handout for all who attend the session.

- *Professional Library.* Provide teachers with a "library orientation" that focuses on the professional materials (both print and nonprint) in the media center.

- *Professional Journals.* Introduce teachers in your school to the professional journals at the middle-school level. Because so few journals were available at her school, one creative media specialist asked the principal and each teacher to bring a professional journal to her workshop to share with other faculty members. The discussion also focused on electronic journals, and she gave teachers an opportunity to examine several electronic journals such as the IRA's *Reading Online*. Faculty members left this short session with knowledge concerning the availability of journals beyond their own special areas of expertise.

- *Selection Aids.* Media specialists take for granted their own knowledge of the selection tools that they use to locate books and other resources. Many teachers are not aware of these professional resources, and they are often thrilled to learn about the selection aids available in their school library media center. You may also want to consider introducing your faculty members to some electronic selection aids.

- *Publishers' Catalogs.* Several media specialists reported that teachers enjoyed learning about these catalogs that we may take for granted. Because we often get duplicates of these catalogs, keep several on hand to give to all attendees as they leave the workshop.

- *Book Reviewing.* This is another bit of knowledge many library media specialists take for granted. Teachers are very interested in hearing about how books are reviewed. Invite a reviewer (a university professor or librarian who reviews YA or professional books for journals) to share information about the review process during your mini-workshop. Also bring several review journals such as *Booklist* and *School Library Journal* for the teachers to examine. As a follow-up, you may encourage teachers to have students write reviews for books they read in class. Such reviews can be compiled into a booklet, or may be published in the school newspaper or on the school's Web site. (For a detailed example, see Kathleen Yaeger's "Student Book Reviews" program description under "Programs for Students" in this chapter.)

- *Book Fair Materials.* Some media specialists arrange for their book fair company to provide a short program for faculty members that focuses on the materials available for the fair. This is usually presented in the media center so faculty members have an opportunity to browse the book fair without students present. Teachers also enjoy hearing about the selection process for the book fair. They welcome a list of the most popular books for children. Some media specialists arrange for the book fair to include professional materials for teachers and parents, and these resources can be highlighted during the presentation.

- *Young Adult Book Awards and Notable Lists.* Media specialists will find background information on these awards at various Web sites for professional organizations highlighted in Chapter 6. For example, the ALA Web site offers a wealth of information on book awards and recommended reading lists. Select the major awards and notable lists, and provide teachers with a brief summary of their history and purpose. Make the most recent award-winning YA books available for faculty members to enjoy.

- *Booktalking.* A workshop for English teachers on the importance of booktalks is usually well received. At the workshop, share tips on booktalking and familiarize faculty members with the resources that provide information concerning good booktalks. One media specialist who offers this mini-program annually commented, "The teachers in my school were excited to learn about the professional books that provide examples of good booktalks."

- *Bookstores.* Invite an owner or a representative of a local bookstore to your school library media center to share information with teachers. For example, at one mini-workshop a bookstore owner shared a list of the "Best Selling YA Books of the Year" with teachers. She also brought along copies and presented booktalks on three of the most popular adult novels.

- *Paperback Book Exchange.* Designate a special week during which faculty members bring their favorite paperbacks to the media center. Give teachers a ticket for each donated book. Then set up the paperback books on rolling carts in the faculty lounge. Let faculty members exchange their tickets for a paperback book. Using the honor system, they can place the ticket(s) in a container that has been placed near the paperback books and choose the book(s) of their choice from the cart.

- *Luncheons, Receptions, Breakfasts.* Numerous media specialists across the nation indicated that faculty interest in the media center increased after being invited there for a special program or activity. Brown-bag luncheons, economical receptions with punch and cookies, and light breakfasts of rolls and coffee are just a few of the events library media specialists use to generate teachers' interest in the media center. To add a professional development component to the event, showcase new professional and children's books.

- *Field Trip Experiences.* Offer field trips after school to special library-related sites such as the district level professional resources library, a local bookstore, or a nearby university.

- *New Resources in the Media Center.* Through a presentation, newsletter, or display, keep the teachers informed about the new resources available from the media center. Take advantage of the opportunity to teach faculty members how to use new software, equipment, or electronic databases. Demonstrate and provide time for hands-on activities with a purpose.

�֍ *Various Contributors*

"What's New in the Media Center"

The contributors for our book suggested the following ways to advertise the professional and student resources available in the library media center:

- When new books arrive, put a memo in teachers' boxes to let them know that a resource of interest to them has arrived.

- Prior to faculty meetings, display new library materials for faculty members to examine before or after the meeting. Several media specialists were pleasantly surprised that teachers sometimes arrived early to browse through the materials.

- Ask the principal to provide a five-minute period at the beginning of faculty meetings for you to advertise new materials.

- Highlight new materials in a special section of the school or media center newsletter.

- Display new professional materials in the teachers' lounge.

- Use a cart for a rolling display of "New Arrivals" in the teachers' lounge.

- Develop a creative "New Arrivals" memo, and send notes to teachers.

- Display titles of new professional materials on a bulletin board in the teachers' lounge.

- Take the new materials of interest to department meetings and share them with faculty members.

- Make banners and place them on the inside of the faculty restroom stalls. Everyone has to go to the restroom some time during the day, and now you will have a captive audience.

PROGRAMS FOR COMMUNITY

Programs are excellent for involving parents and community members in media center activities. Consider various ways of engaging parents. You might share information related to students, such as sharing reference resources for choosing good books. Or, you might contour a program to their own learning development, such as a beginner's Internet search for adults. Involving parents in positive experiences establishes a wonderful rapport with your students' families, and the community at large.

Information About the Media Center

❋ *Charleen Koppi, Rosemount Middle School, Independent School District 196 (Rosemount, Apple Valley, Eagan), Rosemount, Minnesota*

"Media Center Brochure"

    To let parents and students know what her school library media center provides and how they can use it, Char developed a brochure detailing the services that her facility offers. Besides being a great tool for promoting the school library media center, the brochures also give her a way to reach parents with important information that they would otherwise not receive.

    The brochures turned out to be a great way to give parents the home access information for all the media center's online databases. In developing the brochure, Char included the Rules and FAQ sections so parents could better understand how she runs the media center. Char chose to print the brochure in purple, hoping that it would be easily identifiable when parents and students needed to use it at home.

    She distributed the brochures to teachers so they could hand them out to parents during parent–teacher conferences. Teachers frequently tell Char that her brochures consistently elicit very positive responses from parents. Even more important, the brochures impressed her principal, who thought they generated great PR for the school. Next year, Char plans to print the same type of brochure for parents, and also print a modified version for staff.

✹ *Marney Welmers, Tortolita Middle School, Marana Unified School District, Tucson, Arizona*

"Sharing 'Big Six Skills' with Parents"

To develop a framework that could be understood and developed for any project, Marney worked with an intern from the University of Arizona to develop a generic, online research model based on the "Big Six Skills" of Mike Eisenberg and Bob Berkowitz. They compiled packets containing explanations, examples, worksheets, and checklists, and then made them available to the library Web page so parents and students could access them from home.

Because faculty members are adopting the Big Six concepts as guidelines for all research, Marney hopes that this resource will help parents to better understand what is expected of the students and to effectively guide them in meeting their goals as they move through the complexities of the research process. She recommends *Big 6 to Teach and Learn with the Internet*, by Abby S. Kasowitz (Linworth, 2000) as a helpful resource for media specialists interested in a similar project.

Technology

✹ *Karen Toron Cooper, Montgomery Middle School, Montgomery Township Schools, Skillman, New Jersey*

"Tech Night 2000"

"Tech Night 2000" was held at schools throughout the district and offered a way for Montgomery Township Schools in New Jersey to show how far they had advanced in technology within five years. It also provided an opportunity for schools to showcase technology-related projects.

Montgomery Middle School media specialist Karen Cooper hosted the media center portion of Tech Night at her middle school while the classroom teachers hosted their own sections of Tech Night. The event was a schoolwide technology night open to parents, students, and other interested community members. The two-hour event took place throughout the school in the classrooms, labs, and the school library media center. It provided an opportunity for the media specialist to "show off" the technology available in the media center: 15 networked PC computers, 4 OPAC Winnebago Spectrum online catalogs, a television with cable and a presenter for PowerPoint and other computer-related demonstrations.

At the beginning of the school year, computer teachers and media specialists throughout the district worked together to develop a PowerPoint presentation titled "Did You Know That We Have the Following Technology Resources?" This presentation was given in the various media centers, including Montgomery Middle School, on Tech Night 2000. Student and staff "experts" were available and well prepared to answer technology-related questions. There was shuttle bus service available between schools so guests could visit more than one school on this special evening.

Preparation for Tech Night at Montgomery Middle School required that Karen work closely with classroom teachers to prepare students to be the demonstrators and guides.

Teachers agreed to use the same handouts that students had received during media center instruction. The handouts provided step-by-step instructions about searching the Internet as well as accessing periodical and reference databases such as *SIRS Discoverer* and *Grolier Online*.

To prepare for the evening, the guides were given the opportunity to practice their demonstrations. They also created posters that would interest the community and demonstrate access to the district-wide Web sites. For the event the students presented excellent demonstrations of technology-related research and were able to answer the guests' questions. A print handout of the PowerPoint presentation, "Did You Know That We Have the Following Technology Resources?" was available for parents. Follow-up activities to Tech Night have focused on at-home access for the databases and additional workshops for staff on integrating databases into the instruction.

 *Diane O. Davis and Nancy C. Owen, Harry F. Byrd Middle School, Henrico County Public Schools, Richmond, Virginia*

"Parent Technology Night"

In partnership with the PTA, a Parent Technology Night provides parents at Byrd Middle School with an opportunity to learn new computer skills and become familiar with how the students use computers as a tool to enhance their learning. Parent participants had little or no computer experience. The administrators, a library media specialist, and teachers plan the activities and each participates as a trainer. Some of the activities include

- Accessing and surfing the Internet
- Using different browsers
- Using e-mail
- Learning safe home computer use

Various Contributors

"Mini-sessions for Parents"

Various media specialists we visited over the past year recommend the following mini-sessions (20-30 minute workshops) for increasing the media center's visibility with parents and community members.

- *Media center tour.* Schedule three media center tours for parents. Invite parents to attend one of the three tours. By conducting such tours, you will provide an opportunity for parents to get to know you, to become familiar with the resources available for students, and to learn about the library procedures and your expectations for student use of the school library media center.

- *Web sites for parents.* Plan a parent program that focuses on important Web sites that can provide information on books and resources for middle-school students.

The Web sites for professional organizations listed in Chapter 6 provide excellent starting points for this mini-session. For example, ALA's Web site can offer parents a wealth of information on resources that support their children's educational and personal needs.

- *Book fair.* On the first day (or evening) of the annual book fair, host a special program for parents that gives them an opportunity to become familiar with the resources being offered. The book fair company will usually send a representative to conduct the program. Provide refreshments and a period for parents to browse the book fair.

- *Parents as Readers group.* Several media specialists offer a program for parents that is conducted in a similar manner as the "Teachers as Readers" program discussed earlier in this chapter. Refer to this previous program for detailed information about establishing the program and ordering the special kit available through the IRA.

CONCLUSION

Clearly, library media specialists throughout the country are developing exceptional, meaningful, and fun programs for students, parents, faculty members, and communities. The breadth and depth of your own school library media programs have no limits. Like these enthusiastic and innovative contributors, you too can offer riveting programs that place students center stage in events that have the potential to be the most memorable learning experiences in middle school.

References

Armistead, John. *The $66 Summer.* Illus. by Fran Gregory. Minneapolis: Milkweed, 2000.

Berger, Pam. *Internet for Active Learners: K–12 Curriculum Strategies.* Chicago: ALA Editions, 1998.

Booklist. Chicago: American Library Association, 1905- .

Capote, Truman. *The Thanksgiving Visitor.* New York: Random House, 1967.

Carroll, Joyce Armstrong, and Edward E. Wilson. *Poetry After Lunch.* Spring, TX: Absey & Company, 1998.

Cooney, Caroline. *What Child Is This?* New York: Bantam Books, 1999.

Dickens, Charles. *A Christmas Carol.* New York: Bantam Classics, 1999.

Durbin, William. *The Journal of Sean Sullivan, a Transcontinental Railroad Worker.* New York: Scholastic, 1999.

— —. *The Journal of Otto Peltonen, a Finnish Immigrant.* New York: Scholastic, 2000.

Eckert, Allan W. *Return to Hawk's Hill.* Boston: Little, Brown and Company, 1998.

Evans, Earlene Green, and Muriel Miller Branch. *3-D Displays for Libraries, Schools and Media Centers.* Jefferson, NC: McFarland, 2000.

Frank, Anne. *Anne Frank: The Diary of a Young Girl.* New York: Scholastic, 1999.

Gac-Artigas, Alejandro. *Yo, Alejandro.* New Jersey: Ediciones Nuevo Espacio, 2000.

Harris, Carol Flynn. *A Place for Joey.* Honesdale, PA: Boyds Mills, 2001.

Hausman, Gerald. *Tom Cringle: The Pirate and the Patriot.* Illus. by Tad Hills. New York: Simon & Schuster, 2001.

Henry, O. *The Gift of the Magi.* Illus. by Robert Sauber. Morris Plains, NJ: Unicorn, 1993.

Holdsclaw, Chamique, with Jennifer Frey. *Chamique Holdsclaw: My Story.* New York: Aladdin, 2001.

Kasowitz, Abby S. *Big 6 to Teach and Learn with the Internet.* Worthington, OH: Linworth, 2000.

Leslie, Roger. *Drowning in Secret.* [Forthcoming.] Spring, TX: Absey & Company, 2002.

———. *The Success Express.* [Forthcoming.] Houston: Bayou, 2003.

Leslie, Roger, and Patricia Potter Wilson. *Igniting the Spark: Library Programs That Inspire High School Patrons.* Englewood, CO: Libraries Unlimited, 2001.

Lowry, Lois. *The Giver.* Boston: Houghton Mifflin, 1993.

Macaulay, David. *Castle.* Boston: Houghton Mifflin, 1977.

———. *Cathedral: The Story of Its Construction.* Boston: Houghton Mifflin, 1973.

McLerran, Alice. *Dragonfly.* Spring, TX: Absey & Company, 2000.

Mr. Holland's Opus. Directed by Stephen Herek. Hollywood Pictures, videocassette, (145 min), 1996.

Mitchell, Margaret. *Gone with the Wind.* New York: Scribner, 1996.

Murphy, Jim. *The Journal of James Edmond Pease, a Civil War Union Soldier.* New York: Scholastic, 1998.

Naylor, Phyllis Reynolds. *Shiloh.* New York: Dell, 1991.

Paulsen, Gary. *Hatchet.* New York: Simon & Schuster, 1999.

Planet of the Apes. Directed by Franklin J. Schaffner. Twentieth Century Fox, videocassette (112 min), 1968.

Poe, Edgar Allan. "The Raven." In *The Pit and the Pendulum and Other Stories by Edgar Allan Poe.* Illus. by James Prunier. New York: Viking, 1999.

Powell, Randy. *Tribute to Another Dead Rock Star.* New York: Farrar, Straus & Giroux, 1999.

Rice, James. *A Cowboy Night Before Christmas.* Gretna, Louisiana: Pelican, 1990.

Ritter, John H. *Over the Wall.* New York: Philomel, 2000.

Scieszka, Jon. *Math Curse.* Illus. by Lane Smith. New York: Viking, 1995.

Stewart, Sarah. *The Gardener.* New York: Farrar Straus Giroux, 1997.

Thatcher, Kevin J. *Thrasher: The Radical Skateboard Book.* New York: Random House, 1992.

Wallace, Bill. *Coyote Autumn.* New York: Holiday House, 2000.

Waugh, Charles G., ed. *A Newbery Christmas: Fourteen Stories of Christmas by Newbery Award Winning Authors.* New York: Delacorte, 1999.

Williams, Carol Lynch. *Christmas in Heaven.* New York: Putnam, 2000.

Wilson, Patricia Potter. *The Professional Collection for Elementary Educators.* New York: H. W. Wilson, 1986.

Wilson, Patricia Potter, and Ann C. Kimzey. *Happenings: Developing Successful Programs for School Libraries.* Littleton, CO: Libraries Unlimited, 1987.

Wilson, Patricia Potter, and Roger Leslie. *Premiere Events: Library Programs That Inspire Elementary School Patrons.* Englewood, CO: Libraries Unlimited, 2001.

Wood, Audrey. *The Christmas Adventure of Space Elf Sam.* New York: Scholastic, 1998.

Index

About the Authors

Dr. Patricia Potter Wilson is Associate Professor Emerita of School Library and Information Science at the University of Houston-Clear Lake. Before her university position, she served as a teacher and a school library media specialist in the public schools. In 1986 she received a doctorate in education from the University of Houston.

Patricia Potter Wilson

Dr. Wilson is the author of *The Professional Collection for Elementary Educators* (H. W. Wilson Company, 1996) and co-author of *Leadership for Today's School Library* (Greenwood, 2001). Her first book, *Happenings: Developing Successful Programs for School Libraries* (Libraries Unlimited, 1987) was related to programming. Based on this first book, she and Roger Leslie began the current Library Programs That Inspire series, which includes *Premiere Events: Library Programs That Inspire Elementary School Patrons; Igniting the Spark: Library Programs That Inspire High School Patrons;* and *Center Stage: Library Programs That Inspire Middle School Patrons.*

Dr. Wilson has also published numerous articles related to teaching and research in professional journals such as *School Library Journal, Reading Teacher, Journal of Youth Services, Reading Horizons, Teacher Librarian, National Forum of Educational Administration and Supervision Journal, National Forum of Teacher Education Journal,* and *National Forum of Applied Educational Research Journal.*

Among her many honors, Dr. Wilson was selected as the 1999 Distinguished Alumna at University of Houston-Clear Lake, and in 2002 she received the Distinguished Alumna Award from the College of Education at University of Houston. In 1996 she received the prestigious Enron Teaching Award as well as the President's Distinguished Teaching Award at University of Houston-Clear Lake. She was also selected by students and faculty at the University of Houston-Clear Lake for the 1996 Piper Professor Nominee, which honors outstanding professors. She also actively supports her community by serving on various library and literacy boards in the Houston area.

Dr. Wilson has been involved in a variety of leadership roles in her community where she serves on various boards for libraries and charitable organizations. For her volunteerism and service to community, she was recognized at National Philanthropy Day in Houston as one of the "Outstanding Volunteers of 1999," and in 2001 she was selected as one of the "Men and Women of Heart," by the Bay Area Turning Point.

Roger Leslie

Roger Leslie is an author, editor, teacher, writing coach, library media specialist, and book reviewer with 15 years of experience in public education. Before becoming a school library media specialist, he taught all levels of secondary English and creative writing, served as department chairperson, and coached the Academic Decathlon team as well as several University Interscholastic League groups related to the Humanities.

Many of Leslie's early writings came directly from his classroom experiences. He has published numerous educational articles in journals throughout the United States, including *English in Texas, California English,* and *North Carolina English Teacher.* His personal essays appeared regularly in *Texas Magazine,* and three of his latest efforts are anthologized in *Voices of Michigan, Volume 2* (2000); *Volume 3* (2001); and *Volume 4* (2002). Additionally, Leslie is a book reviewer for the Young Adult section of the American Library Association's *Booklist.*

Leslie's major works include novels, history books, biographies, and screenplays. A specialist in motivation and self-esteem building, he is co-author of the forthcoming inspirational biography, *The Hell I Can't,* and visits schools sharing concepts from his other forthcoming book, *The Success Express.* His latest novel, *Drowning in Secret*, will be published by Absey & Company in 2002.

As both a writer and a teacher, Leslie has received many honors. A comic one-act play and his first published book, *Galena Park: The Community that Shaped its Own History* (1993), brought him special recognition and local citizens' awards. He has also received Teacher of the Year awards from such groups as the University of Texas, Texas A&M University, and Houston's North Channel Chamber of Commerce. In 1989 Leslie was the Galena Park Independent School District's Teacher of the Year. He was featured on ABC News's "Teachers Make a Difference," was listed in Who's Who Among America's Teachers (1992–1996), and has been named one of the Outstanding Young Men of America for the past four years.